The High Tide

Collected Poems in Cornish 1974–1999

with English translations by the author

Tim Saunders was born in Northumberland and was brought up in Cornwall. His first book of poetry *Teithiau* was in Welsh and published in 1977. As well as writing poetry he is the author of a range of important articles, essays and translations. These include 'Why I write in Cornish' (*Planet*,1976) and 'Cornish – Symbol and Substance' (*For a Celtic Future*, 1984) His poems have appeared in the anthology *Writing the Wind: A Celtic Resurgence* (1997) and he is the editor with Amy Hale of *The Wheel – An Anthology of Modern Cornish Poetry 1850–1980* also published by Francis Boutle Publishers. In 1998 he was made a Bard of the Cornish Gorseth.

Tim Saunders

The High Tide
Collected Poems in Cornish
1974–1999

with English translations by the author

Francis
Boutle
Publishers

First published by Francis Boutle Publishers
23 Arlington Way
London EC1R 1UY
(020) 7278 4497

ISBN 0 9532388 6 5

Printed in Great Britain by Redwood Books

Tugann na dánta seo dóchas dom go maireann crithir na gCeilteach slán – san fhilíocht ar aon nós – agus cuireann an dóchas sin an-áthas orm.

These poems give me to hope that the fiery intelligence of the Celts is still alive – at least in poetry – and that hope fills me with joy.

Gabriel Rosenstock
Irish poet and translator

Dhÿ'w flÿc'hez ha' dhÿ flÿc'hez ow flÿc'hez.

To my children and my children's children.

Acknowledgements

The poems *Yn Gworor Gwlazgordh ann Gwolow*, *Benen Bennrudh*, *Gelvynak* and *Kÿweithas ann Gërnÿwyon, Dy'Gwoal Byran, 1985*, were first published in the collection of my poems *Benyn Bennrudh*; *Ty ha' My* and *Ann Nown Meur* were published in Thomas Raine Crow's anthology *Writing the Wind*; *Dowr ha' Maen* in the poetry magazine *Visions*; *Mor ha' Nos* in the polemical journal *Kernow*, and *Karol Nos* on the sleeve of the album *An Tol yn Pen an Telynyor*, by the folk group Bucca.

Tim Saunders
1999

Contents

Introduction

I must have been about six when my father first told me that there was a Cornish language. The first years of my life had been spent in Northumberland, Guyana, and points between. There had been narrow streets, the endless sea, canefields and forest. Early on, I became aware that different people spoke in different ways, and that one person did not always understand if you spoke in another person's way. My mother showed me a magic spell: shapes on paper could capture sounds and the sounds could convey feeling and sense. How many sounds were there in the world, how many shapes on paper, how many spells?

Now we were in a town in Cornwall where the huge sky could suddenly melt grey into the horizon. Delabole was a place where men with the deftness of neurosurgeons opened blue rock like a book. The slate quarry there is one of the oldest and deepest in all Europe. Sometimes, the storms along the ridge road were so fierce that we never managed to reach school. We played in windy fields, crawled through brambles and over rubble, and every evening watched tired men walking up from the quarry gates. There was a place at the other end of the town called Pengelly: what did it mean? We said things in one way, and the wireless said them in another. Why was this? The feeling you got at school was that being 'Cornish' was a condition bordering on a complaint. It was better for all concerned to escape from it. But, apparently, there was a Cornish language, just as there was a French language and a Latin language. What could that mean?

Another parish, St. Tudy, in the green country between the moor and Bodmin. Walter Wilcocks, the schoolmaster, slowly asked us what certain names signified: Franco, Hitler, de Gaulle. With a blackboard, chalk, and a lumpy black wireless bought from the proceeds of wartime paper salvage, he opened space and time for us. We learned how our teeth grew, how our families earned a living, and how our world came to be as it was. We learnt how Cornwall came to be, before England and France and all the rest of it. We heard flowing rhythm and resounding rhyme, saw bright images that brought strange light and colour: it would be years before I connected the name of Charles Causley with this finely-crafted poetic delirium. Walter Wilcocks told us about 'Q', Arthur Quiller-Couch, who had portrayed Cornwall and the Cornish better than any historian had contrived to do.

My clergyman father taught me the letters of the Greek alphabet, my mother taught me phrases of Latin and took me through me first steps in

French, and visiting French students brought this language within hearing. Sometimes, when the weather turned, the wireless from the Irish station at Athlone came through stronger than London. You couldn't always understand it, and sometimes you wondered why you couldn't understand 'Pengelly' and 'Trevisquite'. There were lives being lived, people who laughed sometimes but at other times hid all their pain behind bright eyes and still faces. Words ran with the beat of feet and the rustle of pages. You could take a book to the bank of a stream, and read to the accompaniment of voices drifting down from a field high on the slope opposite. Quite by accident, I stumbled upon the Apocrypha, and found the Maccabees. I had already learned to love the stories of both the Jews and the Greeks. Why did Jewish characters in this common story seem to have Greek names? What prompted people to make a stand that risked destruction?

I went to school in England, and suddenly there was a rush of knowledge, a tide in which I had to struggle to keep afloat. And floating along with that tide there was always poetry, Chaucer and Donne, Corneille and Horace and Yeats. Back home for the holidays, I saw a sign in Cornish down at Padstow. Why couldn't I understand it? Pottering around in the Free Library at Bodmin, I came upon *Handbook of the Cornish Language* by Henry Jenner, the intellectual father of the Cornish Revival. Published in 1904, this book told me that Celts were Catholic Monarchists, that the Initial Consonant had Five States, and that a man swearing by the patron saint of another parish might be suspected of a wilful economy of truth.

With my head spinning, I took a dictionary off the shelf and opened *Old Cornwall* magazine at the poetry section. The current number had part of a long sequence by L. R. Moir about the ghosts of a church's founding. A hare, sacrificed by night in secret, spoke of the unheeding onward rush of its life until it suddenly found a meaning through its death: *Y caren lamma dres an un / May hallen gweles oll an bys.* It took me all afternoon to work out that this meant 'I loved to leap over the down / Where I could see the entire world.' From that afternoon, I too had to write poetry. I tried to tackle extracts from the Middle Cornish dramas – the Sacrifice of Abraham, St. Meriasek in Cornwall, and the like, and floundered through textbooks more recondite than an old-fashioned Attic grammar. I tried to string together words and phrases, got them hopelessly wrong, and found the discipline of the seven-syllabled line and the six-lined stanza quite frightening. But still the poetry came, a little more confidently each time.

The landscape of language lies all about us, yet, at the same time, we constantly renew and reshape it in the depths of our hearts. It has a shape, physical properties and patterns of meaning and emotion. Sometimes, there are zones where one language shades off into another, and sometimes there is a dizzying escarpment. There are areas that have been cultivated intensely over the years and generations and centuries, places where the ground is fertile and seems alive of itself. There are other places where storms and floods have devastated everything, and even the ground beneath our feet seems to give way. At a deep, almost geological level that we have still not yet mapped, changes creep onward without our noticing. Misuse and confusion can erode the topsoil.

Sometimes I have written a lot in English, and sometimes a great deal in Welsh, but always in Cornish. Over the past thirty years, I have mislaid or forgotten dozens of the Cornish poems that I wrote, but occasionally one or two will turn up, and there are some in this book. At first, it was mostly free verse, with a good few songs as well. Before the mid-Seventies, Cornish was not a language you heard much outside concerts and ceremonies, and so you needed the poetry to make the world of the language. That often took you into a landscape that looked more like a stage set. And yet, there was work in Cornish that reached the heart, meditative pieces by Edwin Chirgwin, deceptively effortless songs by W. D. Watson, and sparkling lyrics by Mary Royle. Nicholas Williams wrote easily and confidently, sometimes merrily, sometimes sadly, but always compellingly.

To use Cornish in conversation was so unusual as to be remarkable, eccentric even. But even when a younger element began to break all those generations' silence, the poetry did not stop. Poetry is like the international trade in television programmes: the more you import, the more you will export. And it was a poet who made us break that silence. As a boy I had met Dick Gendall when he came to visit relatives in St. Tudy. My recollection is that I was hoeing some weeds at the time. This was the first time that I had been introduced to a Cornish scholar: why was he not *mysterious*? A small, quiet man with a shy smile, he had the look of a practical person rather than a man of letters. You would have taken him for a mining engineer, a head gardener, or a navigating officer.

He had published magazines in Cornish, emigrated several times, and written stories and poems. Initially working with Robert Morton Nance, the Lenin of the Cornish Revival to Jenner's Marx, he had become increasingly dissatisfied with that man's Morris-wallpaper medievalism. He turned more and more to the resources of the Early Modern period: Cornish was still a community language when Cornwall plunged into its precocious Industrial Revolution. The end of the Sixties brought his textbook *Kernewek Bew (Living Cornish)*, the first book to treat Cornish as a language rather than as a cryptic crossword. As we slid into the Seventies, he began to compose songs for Brenda Wooton, whose unfairly versatile voice could encompass everything from Blues to a hymn, via working songs and unashamed agitprop. Through Brenda's voice, Gendall taught us to think and feel in Cornish about love, about our past and future, and about humanity's place in the universe. His words and his music created the sensibility that still sustains us.

Anthony Conran's *Penguin Book of Welsh Verse* led me into a working classical tradition that periodically absorbs new words and styles, new values, new experience. At university in Oxford and Aberystwyth, I stepped into the huge sweep of Irish poetry from the troubled Age of Saints up to the Troubles that were just beginning. During visits to Brittany, where the people and the landscape were so like Cornwall, I heard gloriously long ballads about life, the universe, and the misdeeds of this or that candidate at the last election. Alan Stivell was turning the *Barzaz-Breiz*, a sort of P-Celtic *Ossian*, into a weapon of contemporary struggle. Youenn Gwernig, a friend of the Breton-descended Jack Kerouac, held crowds in quiet subjection with simple pictures of trees, cyder, and the end of the working day.

Searching through the back numbers of Cornish-language magazines I came across poems by a man called Tony Snell. They were measured and clear, depicting incidents in a way that created the feeling in you rather than *telling* you what to feel. He might be alluding to a legend or a historical event, but when you read the poem you were *there*. He had solved one of the problems of Cornish rhyme, too. Because of the regular penultimate accent, there is a dearth of accented rhyming-words. Snell's solution was alternate stressed and unstressed rhyming, with whose aid the poem can do anything from processing majestically to zipping along like Corneille's alexandrines with afterburners. I managed to track him down, living in Oxford. He had just started writing in Cornish again, both measured classicism and deceptively casual song. It emerged that he and Gendall were old friends, startlingly different though their poetic work might be.

The Scottish poet, nationalist and communist Hugh MacDiarmaid was a constant fascination, and my revision timetable fell apart at the opportunity to meet him and Valda Trevlyn, his Cornish wife. (MacDiarmaid was very impressed by Snell's work: 'This is the real stuff' he said in a letter.) A documentary about the Spanish Civil War introduced me to the dark-coloured life and poetry of Federico García Lorca. A rabbi, a friend of my father's, gave me an elementary textbook of Hebrew, and I found myself trying to grapple with the deceptively simple poems of Chaim Nachman Bialik, the father of Modern Hebrew poetry. According to the *University of Wales Guild of Graduates' Biblical Dictionary*, Bialik could not have been writing poetry in Hebrew, because Hebrew was a dead language. I smiled, thinking of Galileo: *nevertheless, it moves...*

In the Wales of the Seventies, every age of Welsh poetry was vividly present, daily brought fully alive. Protest songs alluded to Aneurin and Taliesin, poets of the sixth century. I attended Llanbadarn church where the great medieval Welsh poet Dafydd ap Gwilym, a cross between Ovid and the Archpoet of Cologne, complained that the female members of the congregation were making cruel fun of him. There was Goronwy Owen, who sang like an angel, drank like a fish, and taught humane letters to Thomas Jefferson. Williams-Parry and his cousin Parry-Williams spanned a complete spectrum of the Epicurean and the Stoic. Niclas y Glais preached revolution. Hymn-writers Pantycelyn and Ann Griffiths sang with eyebrow-raising delight of God. Wales' most prolific contemporary writer Bobi Jones offended delicate sensibilities and recast old words, old forms, old meanings. Dafydd Iwan, from a venerable poetic dynasty, was becoming the Robeson of Welsh revolt. Poet, editor, critic and scriptwriter Alan Llwyd was leading the strategic renewal of classical poetic art. It was a time and place that would have made anybody sing – and did.

Much of what I wrote during the Seventies was slipshod and derivative. But there were lullabies, ballads, and drinking songs that seem to have slipped into the repertoire. There was free verse, too, slipping along with the awkward vigour of the new vernacular. There were love and courage to celebrate, yellow light from windows to remember, and distances to span and explore. But this was the prehistoric age before floppy disks, and arts graduates in search of work find themselves moving a lot. There were over a hundred poems in the manuscript volume that I lost some twenty years ago. But copies of the odd poem surface from time to time. It is always pleasant to meet those old friends again.

During the Eighties, I wrote very little poetry, though there was fiction and some journalism in Welsh, and a mountain of journalism in Irish under bylines most of which I have forgotten. But my daughters Gwenno and Anna needed songs and rhymes, and stories as well. And I began translating the Psalms, letter by painfully-slow letter. The full flow came again in the Nineties, this time through precise forms and in fully-articulated moods. The discipline of rhythm and rhyme gave added force to the flow of feeling and the structure of meaning. Now there were new craftsmen working in the field of Cornish poetry. Graham Sandercock was mastering a near-throwaway style, always accompanied by music. Pol Hodge, our first truly vernacular voice in generations, was beginning to draw on the swelling resources of the colloquial register.

Whenever I have thought that I had something to say, I have always found that I left more unsaid. This constant irritation leads in two opposite directions. First, there is an urge to paint on an ever-larger scale, finding new forms and structures. The long poem, after all, contains the genes of the novel, the drama, and the opera. Words point to things, and things bring their words. Sounds bring their colours and flavours, just as children bring their love with them. Front, constrained sounds like *eu* and *w* bring sadness, and so we have *keudh* – 'anguish' and *kwrr* – 'limit'. There are broad, bright and triumphant sounds like *e* and *a*, giving us *mel* – 'honey' and *kana* – 'sing'. There is a a full strong roundness in the *gw* – of *gwynn* – 'white' and *gwelez* – 'see'. Smooth transition from vowel-position to vowel-position can give us a sort of harmonic, as in *ac'hwezydh* – 'lark'. The shift in accent when a syllable is added at either end reshapes the familiar, as in *fordh*– 'road' > *fordhow* – 'roads' > *difordh* – 'roadless'. And then there are the initial mutations, changes to the initial consonants caused by particular words, like the Hebrew dagesh but with a morphological significance. These affect meaning and disclose unexpected harmonies. *Maz* is 'good' and *baz* is 'stupefaction'. *Avon* is 'river', and as a feminine noun softens what follows. If in confusion I let myself go and dive into *avon vaz*, does the shock of the immersion revive me or does it overwhelm my faculties? *Taz* is 'father', but 'my father' is *ow thaz* and 'your father' is *dhâ daz*: the shape changes, but within it the same essence reaches out for different relationships.

Taking a cue from Tony Snell, I found that the couplet with differently-stressed rhymes shifts meaning along as rapidly as the sound. The penultimate accent makes the standard Celtic seven-syllable line fall easily into two parts, so that the motion of sense synchronises with the rhythm:

y'm ledyyth // yn-dan dhorn fel
you will take me // under a cunning hand

In the following line, movement across the caesura again seems to add sense:

yn-honz // dhÿ gwrr dhâ worwel
beyond // the limit of your horizon

But the movement into the second line of the couplet then resolves the question raised by the first, so that apparent response to the action of taking now becomes a parenthesis:

Y'm ledyyth // yn-dan dhorn fel
yn-honz // dhÿ gwrr dhâ worwel.
You take me (under a cunning hand) beyond the limit of your horizon.

Perhaps the greatest delight lies in the *teirlinenn vac'heug* or 'hooked threeliner'. The most famous *teirlinenn* is that recorded by the parish clerk at St. Just in Penwith about two hundred years ago:

An lavar koth yw lavar gwir,
Na boz nevra doz vaz an tavaz re hir;
Bez den heb davaz a gollaz i dir.
The old saying is a true saying,
that good will never come of the too-long tongue;
but a man without a tongue lost his land.

Internal cross-rhyming is introduced, as in the poem *Ann Degenn Driphlyg* –'The Triple Jewel' (see below). This means that a poem can start from a single word – even a single sound – as well as from a single feeling, person or thing. It concentrates colour, feeling, and description like the tiny cut facets of a precious stone, reflecting in precise directions. I take delight in it particularly because precision is that at which I have chiefly aimed.

By way of illustrating different varieties of Modern Cornish, here is a *teirlinenn vac'heug* as I wrote it, together with versions in the 'Phonemic/Common', 'Unified', and 'Modern/Authentic/Traditional' orthographies. I am grateful to Ray Chubb, Richard Gendall, Ken George, Richard Jenkin, Neil Kennedy and Craig Weatherhill for their help in ensuring that the spelling conforms to the conventions of their various schools of thought – although I alone, of course, am responsible for any errors.

An Degenn Driphlyg (Original)

Eîth, naw ha' d*eg* syllabenn sk<u>av</u>;
rimow kudh br<u>av</u> dhÿ'nn skovarn a'bl*eg*:
teir flamm vyw land*eg* a'lÿsk peub keudh kl<u>av</u>.

An Degenn Driflyg (Phonemic/Common)

Eyth, naw ha d*eg* syllabenn sk<u>av</u>;
rimow kudh br<u>av</u> dhe'n skovarn a bl*eg*:
teyr flamm vyw land*eg* a lesk pub keudh kl<u>av</u>.

An Degen Dryflek (Unified)

Eth, naw ha d*ek* syllaben sc<u>af</u>;
rymow cuth br*af* dhe'n scovarn a-bl*ek*:
try flam bew gland*ek* a-lesk pup cuth cl<u>af</u>.

An Degan Drebyl (Modern/Authentic/Traditional)
Eath, nawe ha d*eag* syllabel sc<u>ave</u>;
reemes keeth br<u>ave</u> than scovarn a bl*eag*:
try flam beaw ha wh*eag* a lesk pub plage cl<u>ave</u>.

The Triple Jewel

Eight, nine and ten light syllables;
three fine secret rhymes that will please the ear:
it is three bright beautiful living flames that will burn up every affliction.

Cornish is now growing independently of what anybody can hope to prescribe. Children and adults alike live *into* the language, rediscovering old means of expression and unwittingly creating new ones at the same time. My ear and my eye constantly refresh Cornish for me, and poetry consolidates that renewal and gives it authoritative form. This is how it must be for any language, which every moment dies and is reborn. Language is immeasurably ancient and vitally new every second. It is consciousness, it is life sweeping across a pattern of waves or frozen in marks on a plane surface. And what language is to consciousness, so poetry is to language. There can be no end to the making of songs.

A guide to pronunciation

There is a diversity of opinion about the various forms of Modern Cornish. Alert readers will find in these poems a great deal of the 'Phonemic' or 'Common' spelling and syntax, albeit with strong overtones of 'Unified', while the 'Modern', 'Authentic' or 'Traditional' vocabulary and idiom are far from absent. I hope that the origin and function of each word will be quite clear from its spelling.

Firstly, three small points require some elucidation. The letter z indicates where there was a [*t] sound in the parent Brittonic. Thus we have *mes* 'acorns' but *mez* 'but', and *bys* 'finger' but *byz* 'world'. The diæresis (the mark over a vowel indicating that it is sounded separately) indicates a vowel mutated from */o/*. Thus we have *koll* 'loss' but *kÿlli* 'lose', or *kog* 'cook' but *këgin* 'kitchen'. The presence of the diæresis makes no difference to the pronunciation. The prefix *omm–* indicates the reflexive proper, while the variant *ÿmm–* I use to show a partial semantic shift. Thus we have *ydh ÿmmladhas* 'he fought', but *ydh ommladhas* 'he killed himself'. The circumflex accent distinguishes words of identical sound but different meaning. Thus we have *kog* 'cook' but *kôg* 'cuckoo', *koll* 'loss' but *kôll* 'hazel'. The circumflex, likewise, makes no difference at all to the pronunciation.

As to accent, the stress will be on the penultimate syllable of a word, unless an acute accent indicates otherwise, as in *c'hwaré* 'soon'. In an accented syllable, the musical pitch of the voice is lower. Where there are two separate elements, the stress will be on the second, as in *Penn Sanz* 'Holy Head', alias Penzance.

The following notes on pronunciation are approximations, but will give readers new to the Cornish language a workable impression of the sound of the poems. In colloquial, or informal and everyday speech, there will often be a certain amount of variation.

Vowels (Bogalennow)

Usually, a vowel will be long if there is a single consonant, or no consonant at all, following it. Otherwise it will be short. Cornish vowels are generally clearer and purer than in English.

Sound	*Long*	*Short*
a	Like the 'a' in 'father'	Like the 'a' in 'bat'
e	Like the 'a' in 'make'	Like the 'e' in 'bet'
eu	Like the 'e' in 'pervert' colloquially, like **e**	Like the 'e' in 'the' colloquially, like **u**
i	Like the 'ee' in 'seen'	Like the 'i' in 'pin'
o	Like the 'au' in 'taught'	Like the 'o' in 'cot'
u	Like French 'u' in 'vu', colloquially, like **i**	Like German 'ü' in 'grün', colloquially, like **i**
w	Like the 'oo' in 'book'	Like the 'oo' in 'tool'
y	A sound between **e** and **i**. colloquially, like **i**	A sound between **e** and **i** colloquially, like **e**

Diphthongs (Dywsonennow)

It should be noted that in colloquial speech the diphthongs sound like simple vowels.

Sound	*Formal pronunciation*	*Colloquial pronunciation*
ae	Like the 'i' in 'fire'	Like long **e**
ai	Like the 'ay' in 'day'	
ei	Like the 'ai' in 'complain'	Like long **y**
ew	Like the 'ee' in 'seen'	
ey	Like the 'eye' in 'eye'	Like long **e**
iw	Like the 'u' in 'institute'	
oa	Like the 'ua' in 'accrual'	Like either long **o**, or long **w**
oe	Like the 'oi' in 'poise'	Like either long **w**, or long **o**
ow	Like the 'o' in 'rose'	Like the 'oo' in 'tool'
yw	Like the 'u' in 'institute'	

Consonants (Kÿnsonnennow)

In general a consonant may have three values. The Primary value is the basic, normal sound of the consonant, the Intervocalic value is how it sounds between vowels, and the Final value is how it sounds when nothing follows it. In formal pronunciation there is not always much difference, but there can be considerable variation colloquially. Where the consonant is doubled it is pronounced in full, so that *pell* 'far' is almost *pel–l*, whereas *pel* will sound almost like 'pale'. The pronunciation of some of the double consonants varies a little more, and this is indicated.

Sound	*Formal pronunciation*	*Colloquial pronunciation*
b	Like the 'b' in 'beat'	Final **b** like **p**
ch	Like the 'ch' in 'chip'	
c'h	Like Scots 'ch' in 'loch'	Like a very strong **h**
d	Like the 'd' in 'deal'	Final **d** like **t**
dh	Like the 'th' in 'this'	Final **dh** can disappear
f	Like the 'f' in 'fear'	
fv	Like a hard **v**	Like **f**
g	Like the 'g' in 'get'	Final **g** like **k**
gh	Like a softer **c'h**	Like a strong **h.** Intervocalic or Final **gh** can disappear
h	Like the 'h' in 'horrible'	
j	Like the 'j' in judge'	Final **j** like **ch**
k	Like the 'c' in 'comb'	
l	Like the 'l' in 'let'	
m	Like the 'm' in 'mother'	**mm** like **bm**
n	Like the 'n' in 'not'	**nn** like **dn**
p	Like the 'p' in 'perhaps'	
ph	Like a very strong **f**	Like **f**
r	Like the 'r' in 'race', but trilled	
s	Like the 's' in 'see'	Intervocalic **s** can be like the 's' in 'those'
t	Like the 't' in 'tell'	
td	Like a very hard **dh**	Like **t**
th	Like the 'th' in 'thin'	Final **th** can disappear
v	Like the 'v' in 'very'	Final **v** can disappear
w	Like the 'w' in 'want'	
y	Like the 'y' in 'yet'	
z	Like a very strong **s**	Primary and Final **z** can be like **s**. Intervocalic **z** can be like **j**: **zz** can sound like **chch**

A note on the translation

The prose translations on the opposite page of each poem are by the author himself. They are close literal versions intended to aid understanding and have no claim to any independent literary merit. It is hoped that they will help even the reader with no Cornish to match the sense of the poems to the lines and stanzas of the original texts. The notes that can be found at the end of the volume explain various local, historical and literary allusions, or the circumstances of the poem's composition.

Poems

Ann Pennlanw

(54vez Pedhyzlu Maesow Chassya dhÿ Dhin Wagner, Trev Jarl, Karolynedh Dhyghow, Gwortheren 18vez, 1863)

Du ydh o tonnow'nn lanwez
a-hyz ann gworwel ha'y lez,
gwynn ann traeth kul ma y'ponsonz
a-dreus lestow feuz ha' chonz,
kann ann kribow durewynn
ma y'c'hwevre mîl vizeug ynn,
rudh ann pennlanw hoarnlomm,
mordrosow trenkvog ha' plomm.

Flÿc'hez hen Daz ann Dowrow,
meibyon Iweredh heb gwow,
yn-tdÿnythyz ganz gwaityanz
yn-ghenyz worth sorr mar sanz:
rÿ'dhothyenz kâmm ha' mîlgâmm
dhÿ wolc'hi dhÿ-vaes ann namm
c'hwath a blose'nn gÿsterenn
a-warthev war ann las nenn.
Skianz breic'h ha' nerth ympynn
a'gÿmmere dalghenn tynn
worth dywedh yn karn kledhydh
herwydh gwir ann kazor rydh:
â pywen bÿz yn mîlvloedh
ny'welen byth skoedh worth skoedh
dre'nn oesow pell hag arav
vertu mar gadarn a y sav.

Y'savsonz polz y'nn gworor
yntre'nn tiredh kaeth ha'nn mor
ha' saluzi'nn howl owrdhrudh
a nell aga gwythi rudh:
ÿna'n-jolyv hag antrenk
ydh enragsonz renk ha' renk,
musurdoth yn peub dywdroez,
bywgarenzedh yn peub gwoez.
Y'nn dÿc'hes war ann ammug,
dowdothya'n-skôn i a'wrug
ganz nell froz dhulas avon
yn-un ÿmmsettya a-bon,
glas sewt aga dynyteth
heb namm, heb miken, heb meth,

The High Tide

(The 54 Massachusetts Infantry[1] at Fort Wagner, Charleston, South Carolina, 18 July 1863)

Black were the waves of the tide the length and breadth of the horizon, white the narrow beach where they ran over barriers of fate and chance, shining white the crests of steel foam where a thousand slender bayonets glistened, red the iron-bare high tide, billows of sour smoke and lead.

The children of the ancient Father of Waters,[2] in truth the sons of the Atlantic, begotten by hope, born to so holy an anger: they had come step by thousand steps to wash away the stain that still befouled the constellation on the blue above.[3] It was the knowledge of arm and the strength of brain that would take a taut grasp at last on the hilt of a sword according to the right of a free warrior: if I lived to be a thousand years old I should never see, shoulder to shoulder, through the long and slow ages such mighty manhood making its stand.

They stood for a moment in the marches between the enslaved dry land and the sea, and saluted the gold-precious sun with the vigour of their red veins: then, lively and without bitterness, they advanced rank by rank, a measured speed in each pair of feet, love of life in each one's blood. In the charge on the defences, they quickly doubled their pace with the energy of a dark blue river as they attacked at a run, blue the livery of their dignity, with-

triliw aga banerow
a-uc'h ann tyweuz ha'nn grow.
Yn fysk ha' froth ha' festin
y'tardhsonz war wal ann dhin,
taranow y'ga bannlev
yn-un dhÿglena leur Nev:
yn-despyt dhÿ vyrdh belenn
dre vreic'h, dre golonn, dre benn,
war-yow ann lu a rezas
dhÿ skattya ann gworthrec'h kas
ganz mall dre'nn skeuzow mogdywl,
divlanna dhÿ'nn nos ha'nn nywl.

Pan sevys ann howl ternos
a-uc'h koezwig, traeth ha' ros,
war lergh ann ladhva dhirveur
ydh yze hanter war-leur:
yn-tont a-uc'h ann gworthvur
y'tdonzye, yn-stryg ha' sur,
baner growseug ann eskar
yn mysk ann awelow c'hwar:
heb revronz, aga thÿwlyl
y'ghwrug ann eskar mar vyl
avél atl dhÿ hirgleudh
rag dispres, rag meth, rag keudh,
yn gwaityanz tÿrri spyryz
ann gwir glan er bynn ann byz.

Mez ow' profya mîl dhispres
ny'wrug ann eskar y les,
lemen tynna aer ebrenn
yn korrwynz tynn war y benn:
frankedh c'hweg yn enawel
a'c'hwavas dre braz ha' gwêl,
fudha peub kae ha' dowrlann,
yn vertu gwlyc'hi peub gwann.

Tryg rÿ'vu, tro, war rydhzyz,
rÿ'dovas c'hwynn trenk y'nn yz,
howl rÿ'sevys ha' sudhaz,
kres rÿz askoras kanz kaz,
mez ot lanwez dhidhifyg,
ÿmmc'hwydh mor arta na'dryg,
rei ow' sudhaz dhÿ'nn twyeuz
a'fethas peub hagr feuz:
rudh ann pennlanw hoarnlomm,
mordrosow trenkvog ha' plomm,
kann ann kribow durewynn

out stain, without spite, without shame, the three colours of their flags above the sand and the gravel. In rush and turmoil and haste they burst on the outer defences of the fort, thunder in their cheer shaking the floor of Heaven: despite ten thousand bullets through arm, through heart, through head, on ran the host to smite the hateful oppression eagerly through the smoke-dark shadows, disappearing into the night and the fog.

When the sun rose the next day above forest, beach and heath after the enormous slaughter, half were laid low: arrogantly above the rampart there danced, sprightly and assured, the cross-flag of the enemy amongst the gentle breezes; without respect the enemy threw them so vilely like rubbish into a long ditch for insult, for shame, for affliction, in hope of breaking the spirit of that bright truth against the world.[4]

But in offering a thousand insults the enemy did not do his own good, but rather drew the air of the sky in a crushing whirlwind on his head; sweet freedom as a storm blew through meadow and field, overflowed every hedge and bayou, steeping all the weak in manhood.

There has been, at times, an ebb of freedom, sour weeds have grown in the corn, the sun has risen and set, peace has brought forth a hundred battles, but this is an inexhaustible tide, the swelling of a sea that will not ebb again, men who by sinking to the sand overcame every vicious fate: red the iron-bare high tide, billows of sour smoke and lead, shining white the crests of steel foam

ma y'c'hwevre mîl vizeug ynn,
gwynn ann traeth kul ma y'ponsonz
a-dreus lestow feuz ha' chonz,
du ydh o tonnow'nn lanwez
a-hyz ann gworwel ha'y lez.

where a thousand slender bayonets glistened, white the narrow beach where they ran over barriers of fate and chance, black were the waves of the tide the length and breadth of the horizon.

Kontrewait

A-barth dhÿ gÿweithedh, yn-skav a y droez,
rÿ'wibyas lorel dre nywl ann mitin,
aer lawlan Iwerdhon kÿppár ha' gwin,
lev lent ann gog ow' sÿni a'nn glaskoez
a-hyz ann vownder,[1] *a-hyz ann vownder,*
gwodhnow war welz ow' tÿrri koselder:
c'hwi weisyon stowt, agas pennow yn-bann,
agas trëyz mar jolyv y'gas arrai,
kÿzunywc'h, kÿzunywc'h, dydh kynzza Mei
yn donz heb hobba dhÿ vitin Kalann[2]–,
kneuz tomm war dhur yn mysk ann lug tender,
dur gweskyz y'nn koez a-uc'h ann vownder:
    gwleuth, gwoez, ha' linaz,
            ann gog ha'y froz flows;
    linenn lymm lagaz,
            gwivrennow yn-krows.

Arvogyon yn bagaz, dornow'n-leun dur,
patron kâmmow dre'nn vownder y'n gweonz;
heb menestrothi nâ' c'han aga donz,
y'ga phennow'nn ylow gwylz hag anfur
a-hyz ann vownder, a-hyz ann vownder,
gwodhnow war welz ow' tÿrri koselder:
yn-honz dhÿ dhow vryn, yn kreis gworwel yr
y'ma or ow' teudha'n mysk ann glasnedh,
met ot un gwas yowynk a hynz y vedh,
war ann greunvaen loez y hanw y'n gwelyr;
kneuz tomm war dhur yn mysk ann lug tender,
dur gweskyz y'nn koez a-uc'h ann vownder:
    gwleuth, gwoez, ha' linaz,
            ann gog ha'y froz flows;
    linenn lymm lagaz,
            gwivrennow yn-krows.

War ledr ann koettrumm, dow ganzlath dhÿ-vaes,
a y rowedh y'nn lug y'ma ken gwas yowynk,
y golonn yn-lammwylz ha'y dal yn-slynk,
y vys yn-spavel, gwel yac'h heb dysaes
a-hyz ann vownder, a-hyz ann vownder,
gwodhnow war welz ow' tÿrri koselder:
y'n kudhas diweledh skoez huz ann nos,
hag êv ow' tonez dhÿ'nn gwêl nyhewer,
dre roez ann deil yn-un nivera ster
y'ghwoalyas êv rag tardh dydh ha' gwortos;

Ambush

Light-footed in the company of comrades, a lad has flitted through the morning mist, the rainwashed air of Ireland like wine, the slow-witted voice of the cuckoo sounding from the greenwood *along the lane, along the lane, soles on grass breaking quietness*; you upstanding fellows with your heads up, your feet so lively in your formation, unite, unite, the first day of May,[3] in a dance with no hobbyhorse[4] on the morning of the First Day, *warm flesh on steel amongst the immature undergrowth, steel pressed in the wood above the lane: dew, blood, and nettles, the cuckoo and its stream of nonsense; the sharp line of an eye, cross-wires.*

Armed men in a band, fists full of steel, a pattern of steps through the lane they will weave; without instrumental music or song their dance, in their heads the wild and unwise music *along the lane, along the lane, soles on grass breaking quietness*; beyond two hills, in the middle of a fresh horizon a border is melting amongst the greenery, but here is a young fellow on the way to his grave, on the grey granite it is his name that will be seen; *warm flesh on steel amongst the immature undergrowth, steel pressed in the wood above the lane: dew, blood, and nettles, the cuckoo and its stream of nonsense; the sharp line of an eye, cross-wires.*

On the slope of the wooded ridge, two hundred yards away, lying in the undergrowth is another young fellow, his heart beating wildly and his forehead slippery, his finger still, clear vision with no impairment *along the lane, along the lane, soles on grass breaking quietness*; the invisibility of night's shield covered

kneuz tomm war dhur yn mysk ann lug tender,
dur gweskyz y'nn koez a-uc'h ann vownder:
gwleuth, gwoez, ha' linaz,
ann gog ha'y froz flows;
linenn lymm lagaz,
gwivrennow yn-krows.

Gwask dener ann kneuz un polz war ann dur,
dywedh ann dhonz dhÿ'nn Dydh 'mma Kalann,
ydhn y'ga heizyow'n-un nizya yn-bann,
hun downna ez kwsk peub kwsklÿs ha' kÿfur
a-hyz ann vownder, a-hyz ann vownder,
gwodhnow war welz ow' tÿrri koselder:
trëyz poes yn-un dothya dhÿ woskeuz lomm
a-hyz ann vownder, a-hyz ann vownder,
dastewynn ebrenn yn lagaz c'hwath kler,
war laswelz leith ythó eneb gwodomm;
kneuz tomm war dhur yn mysk ann lug tender,
dur gweskyz y'nn koez a-uc'h ann vownder:
gwleuth, gwoez, ha' linaz,
ann gog ha'y froz flows;
linenn lymm lagaz,
gwivrennow yn-krows.

him as he came to the battlefield last night, counting stars through a net of leaves he watched for daybreak and waited; *warm flesh on steel amongst the immature undergrowth, steel pressed in the wood above the lane: dew, blood, and nettles, the cuckoo and its stream of nonsense; the sharp line of an eye, cross-wires.*

The gentle pressure of the flesh one moment on the steel, the end of the dance on this First Day, birds in their flocks flying upwards, a slumber deeper than the sleep of every opium and drug *along the lane, along the lane, soles on grass breaking quietness*; heavy feet speeding to the sparse cover along the lane, along the lane, the reflection of the sky in an eye still bright, on damp grass a warm face; *warm flesh on steel amongst the immature undergrowth, steel pressed in the wood above the lane: dew, blood, and nettles, the cuckoo and its stream of nonsense; the sharp line of an eye, cross-wires.*

Fenestr ann Huz

Yn fenestr ann huz y'tynnav gworwel
a liwyow'n-un lenwyl ann gwydr yn-fel,
a-dreus ann avein lymna dyw avon
ha' rybdhe dolow glaswelzeug yn-skôn;
dhÿ'nn glas a-uc'h ponn arghanz y'n towlav,
a-is y'nn pann faeth gwea patron brav,
a-dreiv y'pynzellav ergh war warthev,
a-rag y'nn straz evan, korlann, fordh, trev:
Yn fenestr ann huz, yn fenestr ann huz,
hunrozow galloz, glori ha' gwoluz.

Yn fenestr ann huz y'tynnav eneb,
po eneb nâg onen, po eneb neb,
eneb ganoweug lagazeug evan,
ganow'n-leun aer ha' lagaz yn-leun tan;
rÿi hanw dhÿ'nn eneb 'mma y'n mynnav,
hanw yr ann Gweinten po hanw lomm Gwav,
dhÿ'nn lagaz rÿi liw hunroz po hunlev,
dhÿ'nn ganow rÿi geiryow Yfarn po Nev:
Yn fenestr ann huz, yn fenestr ann huz,
hunrozow galloz, glori ha' gwoluz.

Yn fenestr ann huz y'tynnav linenn,
a-dreus, hag onen a woelez dhÿ benn,
ha' ranna'nn fenestr arta c'hwec'hgweîth,
pedrogow peub tu a'vydh, eîth hag eîth;
gwydhboell y'nn fenestr y'n gwaraeav,
war ann eneb ha' war ann tirlun brav,
gwaia gwerin, dÿc'hesi war farys,
war ann meic'hdeyrn marw gworra blein bys:
Yn fenestr ann huz, yn fenestr ann huz,
hunrozow galloz, glori ha' gwoluz.

Yn fenestr ann huz y'ghwelav magoer,
gwulf kneuz yn-dan deudha kÿppár ha' koer,
mog yn-dan froza dre'nn gwydr tÿrryz
ha' lenwyl peub kÿrnnig a'w pharleth glyz;
klywez hanazow dre'nn fenestr y'n gwraav,
gwelez howl gwoliyz yn ebrenn glav
prêst yn-dan gÿlli gwoez war ow leurlenn
yn-skwithyz ha' suger, heb fysk, heb frenn:
Yn fenestr ann huz, yn fenestr ann huz,
hunrozow galloz, glori ha' gwoluz

The Magic Window[1]

In the magic window I shall draw a horizon, filling the glass with colours cunningly, across the picture drawing two rivers, and by them green-grassed meadows quickly; onto the blue above, I shall throw light silver dust, below in the fertile cloth weave a brave pattern, behind I shall brush in snow on a summit, in front in the broad valley bottom, sheepfold, road, town: *in the magic window, in the magic window, dreams of power, splendour and wealth.*

In the magic window I shall draw a face, either nobody's face, or a particular person's face, a big-mouthed big-eyed face, mouth full of air and eye full of fire; give a name to this mouth is what I will do, the fresh name of the Spring or the bare name of Winter, to the eye give the colour of dream or nightmare, to the mouth give words of Hell or Heaven: *in the magic window, in the magic window, dreams of power, splendour and wealth.*

In the magic window I shall draw a line across, and one from bottom to top, thus dividing the window again six times, so that there are squares in each direction, eight by eight; it is chess[2] that I shall play in the window, on the face and on the fine landscape, move pawns,[3] charge at a knight, on the dead king[4] place the tip of a finger: *in the magic window, in the magic window, dreams of power, splendour and wealth.*

In the magic window I shall see a ruin, a rich seam of flesh melting like wax, smoke flowing through the broken glass and filling every cranny of my cosy sitting room; hear moans through the window is what I then shall do, see a wounded sun in a sick sky constantly bleeding onto my carpet, tired and oozing, without haste, without excitement: *in the magic window, in the magic window, dreams of power, splendour and wealth.*

Krogenn Leun ha' Krogenn Wag

Yn kerc'hynn un dywozenn
yn-kann, yn-krÿnn hag yn-trenn,
y'ghwe kreatur tywlvludh
dagrenn rewberfeith ha' kudh:
ydh oel ann mor yn-rindromm
war gonna lyvn ha' tomm,
kÿlli dagrow karenzedh
a-uc'h kolonn byth na'hedh.
Mez estr a'we heb gwortos
yn kerc'hynn kac'hennig blos
lezgronnell glavloez ansplann
krac'hberlenn na'dalvydh mann:
gwoe hi ann ven a's gwiskko
war groghen lyvn ha' kro,
gwodhevyl breinvrath loskvaen,
teudha kneuz yn flaer ha' paen!
Yn flammow beudhez a'vraz;
c'hwerththin rÿ'vo ann marwnaz!

Yn gwonyz gwiw awtorteth
ny'vydh jammes skile veth;
glan y'fvydh lawn ann kledhydh
yn-ghrontyyz ganz gwerin rydh:
owth holya lergh gwiryonedh
peub kâmm bÿz yn ammal vedh
ny'bÿrthyr own a'nn skeuzow
kyn ydh eyr dre dhownnanz gow.
Mez y'fÿ prêst heb gwoskeuz
a'vodhgammo gwir ha' breuz;
y's rÿg ann gwynz ha'nn keseir
a'lokkro lavar ha' geir:
a'hÿlerc'hc'ho kar gwerin
y'skorz ann lughez ann tin.
Yn flammow beudhez a'vraz;
c'hwerththin rÿ'vo ann marwnaz!

Kÿweithedh leil y'nn azwy
a'seiv bÿz pan fallonz mwy,
bomm rag bomm ganz ann eskar
yn-un y drokkya heb mar':
kein kadarn worth kein kadarn,
bysyez yn-tynn war ann karn,
a-wirvodh a'ga growedh
ganz geiryanz meur yn un bedh.

Full Shell and Empty Shell

About one grain of sand, shining-white and round and vigorously will a dark soft creature weave a frozen-perfect and secret tear: the sea will weep with sudden secrecy on a smooth and warm neck, shed tears of love above a heart that will never cease. But oysters will weave without waiting around a foul particle of excrement a sick grey inglorious spheroid, a pseudo-pearl with no value at all: woe to her the maid who wears it on smooth and fresh skin, suffering the putrid bite of sulphur, flesh melting in stink and agony. *Let those who betray drown in flames; may laughter be their elegy.*

In the fitting exercise of authority there is never a cause for shame; clean will be the blade of the sword granted by a free common people: by following the path of truth every step to the verge of the grave there will never be felt fear of the shadows despite going through a hollow deep valley. But constantly flee without shelter whoever willingly distorts rightful judgment; the wind and the hail will tear whoever corrupts saying and word: whoever persecutes a friend of the common people will have their posterior whipped by the lightning. *Let those who betray drown in flames; may laughter be their elegy.*

Faithful friends in the breach will stand until at last they fail, with the enemy exchanging blow for blow undoubtedly: stout back to stout back, fingers tight on the hilt, of

Mez rewez gwoez trenk oeryein
a'wanno kollell dhÿ'nn kein;
teudhez kneuz plos yn leithgrac'h,
yn tôrrow podrez ann kac'h:
dre bennow palez meuryeun,
bydhez garrow boez dhÿ geun;
skwardyer skrizow dhÿ'nn awel,
ha' henwyn dh'ankov koeg fel!
Yn flammow beudhez a'vraz;
c'hwerththin rÿ'vo ann marwnaz!

their free will lying with great fame in one grave. But may the blood of whoever thrusts a knife to the back freeze; may foul flesh melt into damp scab, in bellies may excrement rot: through heads let ants dig, may legs be food for dogs; may voices be torn to the breeze, and names to vacuous underhanded oblivion. *Let those who betray drown in flames; may laughter be their elegy.*

Yn Gworor Gwlazgordh ann Gwolow

Yn gworor gwlazgordh ann gwolow
y'ma dowr ow' kana dhÿ'nn grow;
le pawes ann gwynz rÿ'n trovyas
yn mysk ann gwleuth yr ha'nn deil glas:
ow' c'hwystra c'hwath y'ma gwreidhenn
avorow yn gweryz ow phenn;
yn gworor gwlazgordh ann gwolow
y'ma dowr owth amma dhÿ'nn grow.

Yn gworor gwlazgordh ann gwolow
y'ma gwiwer ow' c'hwilaz know;
le pawes ann skeuz rÿ'n trovyas
yn mysk tonnow rewyz gwelz bas:
ow' c'hwystra c'hwath y'ma lanwez
bloedh c'hwath y'm gwoez sal, lez-ha'-lez;
yn gworor gwlazgordh ann gwolow
y'ma gwiwer ow' kÿntell know.

Yn gworor gwlazgordh ann gwolow
y'ma gwas ow' trec'hevyl krow;
le pawes ann dyn rÿ'n trovyas
yn mysk magoer vyw ann hen blas:
ow' c'hwystra c'hwath y'ma oerwynz
deg myrdh oes na'vu byth gweîth kynz;
yn gworor gwlazgordh ann gwolow
y'ma flammow war oelez grow.

In the Marches of Light's Kingdom

In the marches of light's kingdom water is singing to the gravel; it is a resting place that the wind has found amongst the fresh dew and the green leaves: still whispering is the root of tomorrow in the soil of my head; in the marches of light's kingdom water is kissing the gravel.

In the marches of light's kingdom a squirrel is looking for nuts; it is a resting place that the wind has found amongst the frozen waves of shallow grass: still whispering is the tide of another year of life through the length and breadth of my blood; in the marches of light's kingdom a squirrel is gathering nuts.

In the marches of light's kingdom a fellow is building a hut; it is a resting place that the man has found amongst the living ruins of the ancient palace: still whispering is the icy wind of a hundred thousand ages that have not yet been; in the marches of light's kingdom there are flames on the hearth of a hut.

Tavow

Ot omma dhÿz gwlazgarenzedh
ann losow,
emprwreth allozeug
ann c'hwynn ha'nn spedhez!
Ryb agan kaeow,
a-dreiv agan chÿow,
hag yn mysk agan pailow dov
y'ma nerth gwylz
ann planzow;
luyow ledan bêst
a'vynn dÿc'hesi war agan toyow,
dalghenna y'gan muryow,
ha' potya aga deinz.
Y'ma danjer dhÿn diwreidhya
ha' kowllÿski
ann planzow,
gwul dhÿdhy gwodhevyl
dirloesow muskog
yntre'gan deinz ni.
Dÿnarc'h y'gan bydh
arteithya ha' lÿski,
trÿc'hi ha' moldra,
dÿstrewi –
ha' woze ann aerva,
ann hagr blanzow
a'vynn liva a-dreuson ni
ha'gan treilya
dhÿ'nn dhoar arta.

Touches

Here you have the patriotism of the vegetables, the powerful empire of the weeds and the brambles! By our hedges, behind our houses, and amongst our tame fences is the wild strength of the plants, broad armies of moss that will charge at our roofs, seize our walls, grind them and kick their teeth. We have jurisdiction to uproot and entirely to burn the plants, make them suffer mad agonies between our teeth. We shall be welcome to torture and burn, cull and murder, exterminate – and after the battle, the bloody plants will flow over us and turn us to earth again.

Avalow Mei

(Boregan Galann Mei)

Vossaw dhÿmm, a' wydhenn yr,
aval a'nn par na'vlesyr
    lêmmyn yn gwydhlannow'nn byz
marnaz yn bro (c'hweg hy son)
avalleun bell Avallon
    isworweleug gelgeryz:
        kÿzun gennyv, ha' nâ' lei,
        kÿzunyyn, yn mitin Mei.

Vodya ny'vynnav a'th skeuz
a'w bodh nâ'n-skôn nâ'n-pareuz
    lemen unya beun worth beun;
my ow gwolog a'n uc'hdreil,
aval y c'hwilaz y'th tdeil,
    ympya prenn worth prenn gwresleun:
        kÿzun gennyv, ha' nâ' lei,
        kÿzunyyn, yn mitin Mei.

Veiaj dre'th fvarr lyvn y'n gwraav
a skorr dhÿ skorrenn arav,
    lent y'th tywlgow kloar ha' bas;
mantell dhâ dheil bludh tavlymm
a'w hyz a'froz, a-dro dhÿmm,
    injin dhâ awel wyrdhlas:
        kÿzun gennyv, ha' nâ' lei,
        kÿzunyyn, yn mitin Mei.

The Apples of May

(An Aubade for May Day)[1]

Grant me, sweet green tree, an apple such as is not now tasted in the orchards of the world except in the sweet-sounding far country of Avalon,[2] full of apples, below the horizon and secretly loved: *unite with me, and nothing less, let us unite, in the morning of May.*[3]

I will not willingly leave your shadow quickly or readily, but rather unite tree-trunk to tree-trunk; for my part I shall turn my gaze upwards and look for an apple amongst your leaves, graft wood onto wood full of warmth: *unite with me, and nothing less, let us unite, in the morning of May.*

It is a journey that I shall make through your smooth twigs from branch to slow-moving branch, slow-witted in your cool and shallow darkness; the cloak of your soft, sharp-touching leaves will flow along me and around me, subtlety of your deep green breeze: *unite with me, and nothing less, let us unite, in the morning of May.*

Hunrozores

Y'ma hi ow' kwska,
ha'y leuv owth egina,
ha'y phalv ow' pleuzowa
dre des, dre wleuth.
Worth dywedh y'tdeu
gwenyn dur
adhi-worth Hynz Karr Arthur,
pryvez kann
dhÿ gÿntell peill
yn mysk hy bysyez hir.
Eskylli kosel a'wra amma
dhÿ'nn ewineuz, dhÿ'nn olow-bysyez,
ha' kogara hunlevow
dhÿ golonn ann dalghenn.

Dreamer

She is sleeping, while her hand is shooting forth, and her palm flowering through sultry heat, through dew. At last will come steel bees from the Way of Arthur's Chariot[1], brilliant-white insects to gather pollen amongst her long fingers. Quiet wings will kiss the nails, the fingerprints, and confide nightmares to the core of the grasp.

Pyw a'byow?

Pyw a'byow ann Hav ha'nn Gwav,
ann Gweinten c'hweg ha'nn Kynyav?
Pyw a'byow ann nos ha'nn dydh,
ann mor ha'nn maes ha'nn mÿnydh?
ty ha' my a'byow a'welyn,
ni a'wel war-barth a'byowyn.

Pyw a'byow ann kwsk ha'nn hun,
ann snellvyw skav ha'nn difun?
Pyw a'byow ann gwleuth ha'nn ponn,
hag ewynn lan ann vordonn?
ty ha' my a'byow a'welyn,
ni a'wel war-barth a'byowyn.

Pyw a'byow ann gwoez ha'nn c'hwys,
ha'nn dagrow sal po melys?
Pyw a'byow ann bas ha'nn down,
Avallon las hag Annown?
ty ha' my a'byow a'welyn,
ni a'wel war-barth a'byowyn.

Whose is It?

Whose is the Summer or Winter, the sweet Spring and the Autumn? Whose is the night and the day, the sea and the night and the mountain? *It is you and I who own what we see, it is we who will see what together we own.*

Who owns the sleep and the falling asleep, the swift-moving alive and the awakened? Whose is the dew and the light flying dust and the bright foam of the seawave? *It is you and I who own what we see, it is we who will see what together we own.*

Whose is the blood and the sweat, and the salt or the sweet tears? Whose is the shallow and the deep, green Avalon or the Realm of the Dead? *It is you and I who own what we see, it is we who will see what together we own.*

Le

Ebrenn loez yn kreis Mis Ebryl,
pyskez war ann lynn ow' lemmyl,
gwoskeuz yntre pylyow maenbonz:
hanw ann le 'mma dhÿmm y'n dyskonz.

Levow gwartheg hell y'nn vownder,
kri ann helghgeun hardh y'nn pellder,
kryc'how c'hwamm yn ganow'nn ogov:
dhÿmmo i a'dhysk ma ydh yzov.

Place

Grey sky in the middle of April, fish leaping on the lake, shelter between the piles of a stone bridge: it is the name of this place that they teach to me.

Voices of sluggish cattle in the lane, the cry of the bold hounds in the distance, capricious ripples in the mouth of the cave: it is to me that they teach where I am.

Morreb

Ot omma ma y'rez ann koez
dhÿ'nn traeth war lergh un dhywdroez:
y'nn pryskwydh gwynn y vyz neb
a'dhewis hynz ann morreb,
gwynn y vyz tywl neb a'bon
dre'nn skeuzow war lergh gwreic'hyon:
flamm wyrdh, tonn rudh, dyw elvenn,
lanwez ha' tryg diworphenn.

Ot omma ma y'kerdhas tan
bÿz min ann ewynn gannlan:
war benn pan dhieskynn flamm,
pan dremmyn gwynz a-garlamm,
y'rez ann gwoez tonn ha' tonn
ha' fudha gworwel kolonn:
flamm wyrdh, tonn rudh, dyw elvenn,
lanwez ha' tryg diworphenn.

Ot omma ammal ann byz,
ot omma fin ann formyyz:
gwreyn byrla ann lanwez sanz
ha' neuvya yn mor gwordhyanz,
ponya heb hokkyanz, heb kel,
trÿi eneb dhÿ'nn enawel:
flamm wyrdh, tonn rudh, dyw elvenn,
lanwez ha' tryg diworphenn.

By the Sea

Here is where the wood runs to the beach after a certain pair of feet: amongst the brushwood happy is he who will choose the path by the sea, darkly happy[1] he who will run through the shadows after sparks: *green flame, red wave, two elements, unfinished flow and ebb.*

Here is where fire walked to the verge of the bright shining foam: when a flame descends onto a head, when wind passes at a gallop, the blood will run wave upon wave and overflow the horizon of a heart: *green flame, red wave, two elements, unfinished flow and ebb.*

Here is the edge of the world, here is the limit of the created: let us embrace the holy tide and swim in the sea of praise, run without hesitation, without concealment, turn a face to the storm: *green flame, red wave, two elements, unfinished flow and ebb.*

Liwyow

Melynn tyweuz ryb ann glasvor,
melynn gwolow fenestr agor,
melynn deil worth dalleth Kynyav,
melynn gwora, melynn kalav.

Gwyrdh ann deil yn Mis Gwortheren,
gwyrdh ann gwelz ha' gwyrdh Berlewen,
gwyrdh ann mor ha' leun a wolow,
gwyrdh eginenn, gwyrdh avalow.

Rudh ann gwin ma y'ghansoz bardhas,
rudh ann rôsenn wylz a'wywas,
rudh ann tan nosweîthyow Genveur,
rudh ann gwoez a'vu war gazleur.

Colours

Yellow sand by the green sea, yellow light of an open window, yellow leaves at the beginning of Autumn, yellow hay, yellow straw.

Green the leaves in July, green the grass and green Venus, green the sea and full of light, green a shoot, green apples.

Red the wine where poetic art was born, red the wild rose that withered, red the fire on January nights, red the blood that was on a battleground.

War Woen Las[1]

Pur ha' pell
ann wylan wynn hy askell,
bleuzenn bluveug ann salwoen,
yn-leun a haz havow gwell.

Tonnow tynn
rÿ'droc'has dre vur ewynn,
meirc'h meur heb spral nâ' c'hadoen
a-garlamm dhÿ vin traeth gwynn.

Skath mar skav
owth araz maes yn-arav,
gwylz ann ar gwyrdh a'azwoen,
faeth heb yz nâ' foen a'sav.

On a Green Down[2]

Pure and distant the white-winged sea-gull, the feathery flower of the salty down, full of the seed of better summers.

It is tense waves that have cut through a wall of foam, great horse without hobble or chain galloping to the edge of a white beach.

A boat so light slowly ploughing a field, wild the green tilth that it knows, fertile without corn or hay standing.

Ann Edhn Tan[1]

Skon ha' skav
war fordhow nev y'nizav:
flamm ow phluv dre'nn fyrmament
ow' sia a sÿrryanz brav.

Fîn ha' fell
y'lÿsk ow thoth dywaskell:
luzw a lergh pell ow entent
worth tu ha' gworwelow gwell.

Frank ha' fraeth
ow gwibyow gwylz dre'nn alaeth:
yr ann owr y'm koedh anlent,
flowrra flamm rydh ez dydh kaeth.

Pan rogav pann ann ebrenn dywl,
ann nos pan y'm tÿwl yn un polz splann,
ny'voraethav mann pan vyrlav ann nywl.

The Fire Bird

Swiftly and lightly on the roads of heaven
I shall fly: the flame of my feathers
through the firmament humming with a
fine anger.

Finely and cruelly my speed will burn
wings: ash distantly tracing my endeavour
towards better horizons.

Unencumbered and fluent my wild
swoops through the galaxy: dewy-fresh
the gold in my quick-witted fall, a free
flame surpassing an enslaved day.

When I rend the cloth of the dark sky,
when the night throws me down in one
bright moment, I shall not mourn at all
when I embrace the mist.

Yn Lannerc'h Gudh y'nn Glaskoez

Yn lannerc'h gudh y'nn glaskoez,
y'nn koez yn-dan dheil gwyrdhlas,
y'nn argel 'na ny'worras
marnazo êv y dhywdroez.

Pan welis dhâ daz-bezydh,
ha'nn gwydh yn-dan dheil nëwydh,
y'roas êv dhÿmm dow lyther hir
dhÿ'th fvrëdyr wir ha'th c'hwëyrydh.

Yn lannerc'h gudh y'nn glaskoez,
y'nn koez yn-dan dheil gwyrdhlas,
y'nn argel 'na ny'worras
marnazo êv y dhywdroez.

Dhÿ'th fvrÿdyr c'hweg y'skrivas
dyskaz rag dyski bardhas,
hag onen rag gwea kota brav
er bynn ann Gwav mar ac'has.

Yn lannerc'h gudh y'nn glaskoez,
y'nn koez yn-dan dheil gwyrdhlas,
y'nn argel 'na ny'worras
marnazo êv y dhywdroez.

Dhÿ'th c'hwëyrydh y'nn Tir Uc'hel
y'tdyskas teudha'nn awel,
morthoelya'nn aer dhÿ lawnow sur
rag arvow dur dhÿ vresel.

Yn lannerc'h gudh y'nn glaskoez,
y'nn koez yn-dan dheil gwyrdhlas,
y'nn argel 'na ny'worras
marnazo êv y dhywdroez.

Ha' dhÿz y'fvynn êv danvon
geir huz heb son nâ' dasson
a'drec'h ann rei a'th kas a-bell,
eskereinz gall ha' ladron.

Yn lannerc'h gudh y'nn glaskoez,
y'nn koez yn-dan dheil gwyrdhlas,
y'nn argel 'na ny'worras
marnazo êv y dhywdroez.

In a Secret Glade in the Greenwood

In a secret glade in the greenwood, in the wood under verdant leaves, in that retreat none but he have set their feet.

When I saw your godfather, when the trees were under new leaves, he gave me two long letters for your true brothers and your sisters.

In a secret glade in the greenwood, in the wood under verdant leaves, in that retreat none but he have set their feet.

For your sweet brothers he wrote one lesson to teach the art of poetry, and one for weaving a fine coat against the winter so vicious.

In a secret glade in the greenwood, in the wood under verdant leaves, in that retreat none but he have set their feet.

To your sisters in the High Country[1] he taught the melting down of the breeze, hammering the air into dependable blades for steel weapons for war.

In a secret glade in the greenwood, in the wood under verdant leaves, in that retreat none but he have set their feet.

And to you he will send word of magic without sound and echo that will defeat from afar those who hate you, devious enemies and thieves.

In a secret glade in the greenwood, in the wood under verdant leaves, in that retreat none but he have set their feet.

Kerdhez dre'th Fvywnanz

Kerdhez dre'th fvywnanz, eur lent hag eur,
dhÿ b'le ny'woedhes, dhÿ b'le ny'th tdeur.

C'hwilaz ha' c'hwilaz gworwel nëwydh,
c'hwilaz brëdyredh, c'hwilaz c'hwëyrydh,
c'hwilaz ann mo ha' c'hwilaz ec'hwedh,
c'hwilaz c'hwëyrydh, c'hwilaz brëdyredh.
Kerdhez dre'th fvywnanz, eur lent hag eur,
dhÿ b'le ny'woedhes, dhÿ b'le ny'th tdeur.

Holya ha' holya lergh ann mitin,
holya kylc'hdro, holya loerewin,
holya tramor, holya dre'nn vammvro,
holya loerewin, holya kylc'hdro.
Kerdhez dre'th fvywnanz, eur lent hag eur,
dhÿ b'le ny'woedhes, dhÿ b'le ny'th tdeur.

Trovya ha' trovya penn ann troezlergh,
trovya yn tes, trovya yn poesergh,
trovya'nn gan ha' trovya'nn ganores,
trovya yn ergh, trovya yn poestes.
Kerdhez dre'th fvywnanz, eur lent hag eur,
dhÿ b'le ny'woedhes, dhÿ b'le ny'th tdeur.

Walking through your Life

Walking through your life, slow hour by hour, to where you do not know, to where you do not care.

Searching and searching for a new horizon, searching for brothers, searching for sisters, searching for the time before the dawn and searching for the late afternoon, searching for sisters, searching for brothers.
Walking through your life, slow hour by hour, to where you do not know, to where you do not care.

Following and following the track of the morning, following an orbit, following a fingernail of moon, following beyond the sea, following through the motherland, following a fingernail of moon, following an orbit.
Walking through your life, slow hour by hour, to where you do not know, to where you do not care.

Finding and finding the end of the footpath, finding in summer warmth, finding in heavy snow, finding the song and finding the singer, finding in snow, finding in heavy summer warmth.
Walking through your life, slow hour by hour, to where you do not know, to where you do not care.

Dowr ha' Maen

Dowr a'dhewis hynz ann nanz
ma y'tdÿg c'hwythennow bywnanz;
karn loez purbaz haen ha' haen
war warthev y'n fwnd greunvaen:
dowr ha' greunvaen, greunvaen, dowr,
kÿtteudha ny'n gwraonz skantlowr;
glawenn war hirvaen a'bon,
grow a'slynk a-hyz avon:
dowr dhÿ'nn bleuzow, maen dhÿ'nn gwreidh,
my dhÿ'nn lowarn, ty dhÿ'nn bleidh.

Bleuzow a'dhewis ann aer
ma y'tdonzyonz fêst yn-skavdaer;
sosten heb festin nâ' frenn
a'nn pri y'n sugn ann wreidhenn:
bleuzenn, gwreidhenn, gwreidh ha' bleuz,
rÿi ha' resseva gwoskeuz;
briallen dhÿ'nn dydh a'dardh,
y'nn downder, gwreidh a'vinc'hwardh:
dowr dhÿ'nn bleuzow, maen dhÿ'nn gwreidh,
my dhÿ'nn lowarn, ty dhÿ'nn bleidh.

Bleidh a'dhewis ann jass goth
ma ydh helgh ann gam del dhÿgôth;
dre nanzow, war hal, ryb karn,
a-lez y'ghwandr ann lowarn:
Bleidh ha' lowarn, lowarn, bleidh,
fattel dhiank ann kÿzbreidh?
bleidh a-dreus lannerc'h a'rez,
lowarn a'leimm a'nn spedhez:
dowr dhÿ'nn bleuzow, maen dhÿ'nn gwreidh,
my dhÿ'nn lowarn, ty dhÿ'nn bleidh.

Water and Stone

It is water that will choose the path of the valley where bubbles will carry life; a grey cairn that eternity lays down layer by layer on a summit: water and granite, granite, water, they will scarcely melt together; a rain drop on a menhir will run, gravel will slide along a river: *water to the flowers, stone to the roots, I to the fox, you to the wolf.*

It is flowers that will choose the air where they will dance with much light eagerness; it is nourishment, unhurried and excited, that the root will suck from the clay: flower, root, roots and flowers, giving and receiving shelter; a primrose into the day will burst, in the depths, roots will smile: *water to the flowers, stone to the roots, I to the fox, you to the wolf.*

It is a wolf that will choose the old hunting-ground where it will hunt the game as is fitting; through valleys, on moor, by cairn, far and wide will the fox wander: wolf and fox, fox, wolf, how will the common prey escape? A wolf across a clearing will run, a fox will leap from the briars: *water to the flowers, stone to the roots, I to the fox, you to the wolf.*

Amser

Nynz hedhas ann gwydh ganz tÿvi, nynz hedhas,
nynz hedhas ann streth ganz froza, nynz hedhas,
'ma'nn amser ow' slynkya dhÿ-vaes,
'ma'nn amser ow' slynkya dhÿ-vaes,
pez gwelzenn a'dÿv war ann bryn?
pez eur rÿ'niversoz dhÿn?

Nynz hedhas ann deil ganz gwywa, nynz hedhas,
nynz hedhas ann lynn ganz froza, nynz hedhas,
'ma'nn amser ow' slynkya dhÿ-vaes,
'ma'nn amser ow' slynkya dhÿ-vaes,
pez kâmm bÿz dhÿ warthev ann bryn?
pez eur rÿ'niversoz dhÿn?

Nynz hedhas ann moar ganz pÿdri, nynz hedhas,
nynz hedhas ann tryg ganz kilya, nynz hedhas,
'ma'nn amser ow' slynkya dhÿ-vaes,
'ma'nn amser ow' slynkya dhÿ-vaes,
pez forlenn rÿ'davas ann bryn?
pez eur rÿ'niversoz dhÿn?

Time

The trees have not stopped growing, they have not stopped, the stream has not stopped flowing, it has not stopped, *the time is slipping away, the time is slipping away*. How many blades of grass will grow on the hill? How many hours have been counted out to us?

The leaves have not stopped withering, they have not stopped, the lake has not stopped freezing, it has not stopped, *the time is slipping away, the time is slipping away.* How many steps right up to the top of the hill? How many hours have been counted out to us?

The berries have not stopped rotting, they have not stopped, the ebb has not stopped retreating, it has not stopped, *the time is slipping away, the time is slipping away.* How many eddies have touched the hill? How many hours have been counted out to us?

Lywyaz[1] ann Ebrenn

Glas a gler
hynzi hir yn evander;
ynysow nos y'nn howlwynn,
helghya styr owth holya ster.

Fraeth a froz
lanwezow liw yn hunroz;
tonnnow tener diewynn,
kloar awelow joi ha' kloz.

Skethrow skeuz,
tywlder kÿppár ha' tyweuz;
linenn wolow a-eskynn,
fîn yn-un dhelinya feuz.

Mÿneg py was, lavar dhÿmm pyw
a'gÿmmer lyw peub rudh ha' peub glas
a-dreus mor anvas ann gwolowder gwyw.

The Helmsman of the Sky[2]

Bluely light-coloured long paths in space; islands of night in the sunshine, hunting for meaning by following stars.

Fluent a stream of colour's tides in a dream; gentle foamless waves, cool breezes of delight and praise.

Splinters of shadow, darkness like sand; a line of light rising, finely drawing fate.

Tell what fellow, say to me who will take the helm of every red and green across a sea, by no means shallow, of fading light.

Vodya

Monez yn-kerdh pan dheu gworthewer,
meyn ow' kwska yn fosow isel,
edreg ow' c'hwystra'n-kosel, kosel,
avowa kÿvrin dhown dhÿ'nn gewer.

Kerdhez war fordh a-hyz ann morreb,
meyn ow' kwska dhÿ woelez avon,
lanwez gov ow' puthi peub bystyon,
gwovynn heb gwaityanz kavoz gwortheb.

Gwortos ha' miraz worth ann mordan,
meyn ow' kwska yn mysk ann tyweuz,
gevyanz nowneug ow' c'hwilaz pec'heuz,
gwolsowez worth ann nos polz byc'han.

Kilya a'nn traeth, a'nn tir, a'nn Noarvyz,
meyn ow' kwska yn kylc'how'nn ebrenn,
kov ow' fellyl, kÿvrenn ha' kÿvrenn,
c'hwilaz korfow'nn lavarow kÿllyz.

Departing

Setting out when evening comes, stones sleeping in low walls, regret whispering quietly, quietly, admitting a deep secret to the weather.

Walking on a road along by the sea, stones sleeping at the bottom of a river, memory's tide swamping all dirty water, asking without hoping to get an answer.

Waiting and looking at the fluorescence on the sea, stones sleeping amongst the sand, hungry forgiveness looking for sin, listening to the night for a little moment.

Retreating from the beach, from the land, from the Earth, stones sleeping in the circles of the sky, memory failing, link by link, looking for the bodies of the lost words.

Ty Arloedh Gwynn

Ty Arloedh gwynn, y'th ghwordhyav a'w lev,
a leun golonn, ty Veic'hdeyrn ann Nev.

Rÿ'th ghwormolas ann nevez ha'nn lann,
rÿ'th ghwormollo dowr yntre dywlann;
rÿ'th ghwormolas ann dheilenn war brenn,
rÿ'th ghwormollo lyvr ha' skrivenn:
rÿ'th ghwormolas hen Abram benn krez,
rÿ'th ghwormollo klywez ha' gwelez;
rÿ'th ghwormolas ann broder ha'nn taz,
rÿ'th ghwormollo mÿnydh ha' gwastaz!

Dhÿz, neb yn glawenn rÿ'gronnas liw,
roez peub tra formyyz hy gwordhyanz gwiw!

Rÿ'th ghwormolas ann bara ha'nn gwin,
rÿ'th ghwormollo ann mo ha'nn mitin;
rÿ'th ghwormolas ann sterenn ha'nn loer,
rÿ'th ghwormollo doargae ha' magoer:
rÿ'th ghwormolas ann oelez ha'nn tan,
rÿ'th ghwormollo melys ha' holan;
rÿ'th ghwormolas ann lanwez ha'nn traeth,
rÿ'th ghwormollo dagrow ha' hiraeth!

Dhÿz, neb yn glawenn rÿ'gronnas liw,
roez peub tra formyyz hy gwordhyanz gwiw!

Rÿ'th ghwormolas pryeryn ha' sanz,
rÿ'th ghwormollo maendrumm ha' koeznanz;
rÿ'th ghwormolas tir gwelz ha' tir moel,
rÿ'th ghwormollo kentrow ha' morthoel:
rÿ'th ghwormolas ann gwoendir ha'nn koez,
rÿ'th ghwormollo salmydh ha' profoez;
rÿ'th ghwormolas ann euryow ha'nn dydh,
rÿ'th ghwormollo mammow ha' c'hwëyrydh!

Ty Arloedh gwynn, y'th ghwordhyav a'w lev,
a leun golonn, ty Veic'hdeyrn ann Nev.

You Blessed Lord[1]

You blessed Lord, I shall praise you with my voice, with a full heart, you King of Heaven.

The sanctuary and the churchyard have praised you, may water between two banks praise you; the leaf on a tree has praised you, may book and writing praise you: ancient Abraham, head of faith, praised you, may hearing and seeing praise you; the brother and father have praised you, may mountain and plain praise you.

To you, who in a raindrop has gathered up colour, let every created thing give its fitting praise!

The bread and the wine have praised you, may the time before dawn and the morning praise you; the star and the moon have praised you, may earthwork and ruin praise you: the hearth and the fire have praised you, may the sweet and the salt praise you; the tide and the beach have praised you, may tears and longing praise you.

To you, who in a raindrop has gathered up colour, let every created thing give its fitting praise!

The pilgrim and saint have praised you, may the stony ridge and wooded valley praise you; the grassland and bare land have praised you, may the nails and hammer praise you: the downland and wood have praised you, may the psalmist and prophet praise you; the hours and the day have praised you, may mothers and sisters praise you.

You blessed Lord, I shall praise you with my voice, with a full heart, you King of Heaven.

Geni Flamm

Dhÿ'w phezadow y'roav sel
omma y'nn skeuzow kosel,
war brederow bera koer
ryb nevez ma y'fvu magoer;
a-rag ann hen dhelw prenn
my a'vynn gwonyz tanenn,
yntr' ofygow planza haz
ha' gwortos seson trevaz:
kyn na'm beus skianz nâ' phoell
dhÿz ydh enawav kantoell.

A y dhassorc'h yn lommder teg,
Krist yn glori war wareg,
skeuz oesow down war ann mur,
termynn yn-honz dhÿ vusur;
dyew awel a-vaes y'nn gwydh,
purbaz yn peub polz nëwydh,
roez wolow a-dreus ann nenn
yn-tÿwlyz trank heb gworphenn:
kyn na'm beus skianz nâ' phoell
dhÿz ydh enawav kantoell.

Skeuz ha' skeuz y'tremmen eur,
lanwez lent a-dreus maenleur,
yn-kosel y'tdonz ann flamm
kolonnlamm ha' kolonnlamm;
hy c'han a'wandr heb son
dre'nn pellder palz yntredhon
bÿz ma y'klywyth, yn tro tryg,
keurgan donnow ann ofyg:
kyn na'm beus skianz nâ' phoell
dhÿz ydh enawav kantoell.

Birth of a Flame

To my praying I shall give a seal here in the quiet shadows, on thoughts letting drops of wax fall by a sanctuary where there was a ruin; it is I who will cultivate a spark of fire, between offices plant seed and wait for a harvest season: *although I have neither knowledge or sense, for you I shall light a candle.*

Arisen in beautiful starkness, Christ in splendour on an arch, shadow of deep ages on the wall, a time beyond measure; rustle of breeze outside in the trees, eternity in every new moment, net of light across the ceiling thrown age without finish: *although I have neither knowledge or sense, for you I shall light a candle.*

Shadow by shadow an hour will pass, slow tide across a stone floor, quietly the flame will dance heartbeat by heartbeat; its song will roam soundlessly through the thick distance between us until you hear, in the turn of the ebb, the chant of the waves of the office: *although I have neither knowledge or sense, for you I shall light a candle.*

Karol Nos

Ot omma ni a-rag a's chÿ
un nosweîth yein y'nn Gwav:
oc'h! rÿwc'h dhÿn ni un banne gwin
dh'y eva a'gan sav!

Un banne gwin, un deisenn domm,
y's këgin ryb ann tan:
ha' bydhez dhÿwc'h didhander meur
ow' klywez agan kan!

A venestrothi ha' kan c'hweg
a's chÿ y'n lenwyn oll:
oc'h! lenwwc'h agan tôrrow gwag
po'nnn eil ydh eyn dhÿ goll!

Rÿ'nizzo trëyz a-dreus ann leur,
dhÿwc'h bydhez sosten fîn:
hag er na'saffo arta'nn howl,
rÿ'frozzo kan ha' gwin!

Night Carol[1]

Here we are in front of your house one cold night in the Winter: oh, give us one drop of wine to drink as we stand.

One drop of wine, one warm cake, in your kitchen by the fire: and may you have great diversion hearing our song.

With instrumental music and sweet song we shall fill all your house: oh, fill our empty bellies or we shall be lost.

May feet fly across the floor, may you have fine food: and until the sun rises again may song and wine flow.

Kÿzgana, Korev, Mog

Eva bÿz y'nn gwoelez,
peub banne gelyz glan;
levow oll kÿntellez
yn bwrdhen berr ann gan:
kÿzgana, korev, mog;
moroenyon teg ha' drog.

Dalleth ann gworthewer
ow' slynkya bÿz y'nn nos;
lev mar skov ha' tener–
gwolsowyn worti, 'sos!
kÿzgana, korev, mog;
moroenyon teg ha' drog.

Ynys grÿnn ann gwolow
yn kreis tywlezyon byw;
kan yn skeuz avorow–
ot kolonn yn-dan vryw!
kÿzgana, korev, mog;
moroenyon teg ha' drog.

C'hwardhow, c'hystrow, hanaz,
nenn isel, parwyz lomm;
dagrenn yei yn lagaz,
keudh kudh yn minc'hwardh tromm:
kÿzgana, korev, mog;
moroenyon teg ha' drog.

Singing Together, Beer, Smoke

Drinking right to the bottom, every drop quite gone; all the voices of an audience in the short refrain of the song: *singing together, beer, smoke; beautiful and bad girls.*

The beginning of the evening slipping into the night; a voice so rich and gentle – let's listen to her, boys: *singing together, beer, smoke; beautiful and bad girls.*

The round island of the light in the middle of living darkness; a song in the shadow of tomorrow – here is a bruised heart: *singing together, beer, smoke; beautiful and bad girls.*

Laughter, whispering, moaning, low ceiling, bare wall; tear of ice in eye, secret anguish in a sudden smile: *singing together, beer, smoke; beautiful and bad girls.*

Gwolow Kynzza Gwener

Ganz gwolow kynzza Gwener 'dh aeth ann tren,
ganz gwolow kynzza Gwener 'dh aeth ann tren;
pan dardhas gwolow Gwener,
y'torras tromm ann gewer,
ganz gwolow kynzza Gwener 'dh aeth ann tren.

Ganz gwolow kynzza Gwener 'dh aeth ann tren,
ganz gwolow kynzza Gwener 'dh aeth ann tren;
dre yeinder, glaw ha' gwynzow,
tremmena 'wrug a-gynzow,
ganz gwolow kynzza Gwener 'dh aeth ann tren.

Ganz gwolow kynzza Gwener 'dh aeth ann tren,
ganz gwolow kynzza Gwener 'dh aeth ann tren;
y'tremmen Hav ha' Kynyav,
mez nefra ny'dhÿc'hwelav,
ganz gwolow kynzza Gwener 'dh aeth ann tren.

Ganz gwolow kynzza Gwener 'dh aeth ann tren,
ganz gwolow kynzza Gwener 'dh aeth ann tren;
y'tremmen Gwav ha' Gweinten,
nâ' mwy ny'vydhav lawen,
ganz gwolow kynzza Gwener 'dh aeth ann tren.

The First Light of Friday[1]

With the first light of Friday the train went,
with the first light of Friday the train went;
when the light of Friday broke, the weather
broke suddenly, with the first light of Friday
the train went.

With the first light of Friday the train went,
with the first light of Friday the train went;
through coldness, rain and winds, it passed
just now, with the first light of Friday the train
went.

With the first light of Friday the train went,
with the first light of Friday the train went;
Summer and Autumn will pass, but I shall
never return, with the first light of Friday the
train went.

With the first light of Friday the train went,
with the first light of Friday the train went;
Winter and Spring will pass, but I shall not be
happy any more, with the first light of Friday
the train went.

Amsergan

Meurth ha' Merc'her, Merc'her, Yow,
nos ow' koedha war ann pow:
Gwener, Sadorn, Sul ha' Lun,
kwsk yn kres, ow ydhnig, hun!

Dydhweîth, nosweîth, dydh ha' nos,
gwleuth ow' c'hwystra war ann ros:
nosweîth, dydhweîth, nos ha' dydh,
howl a'seiv ha' howl a'sudh.

Gwav ha' Gweinten, Kynyav, Hav,
bydhez dhÿz hunrozow brav:
ergh hag awel, howlwynn, glaw,
taw dhÿmm polz, ow baban, taw!

Timesong[1]

Tuesday and Wednesday, Wednesday, Thursday, night falling onto the country; Friday, Saturday, Sunday and Monday, sleep in piece, my little bird, fall asleep.

Daytime, night-time, day and night, dew whispering on the heath; night-time, daytime, night and day, sun rises and sun sets.

Winter and Spring, Autumn, Summer, may you have fine dreams; snow and breeze, sunshine, rain, just be quiet for a moment, my baby, be quiet.

Ann Lew

Heb flac'hell nâ' stradal
    ann lew a'a dhÿ-goll
ow' kwandra'nn albanal
    dre'nn dydh ha'nn nos oll;
dre'nn tywlder heb gwaityanz
    y lost êv a'n sew,
heb krib dh'y dhowabranz
    nâg eskov dh'y vlew.

The Lion[1]

Without a flashlamp or a streetmap the lion will get lost as he wanders the sewers throughout the day and all the night. Through the darkness without hope he will follow his tail, without a comb for his eyebrows or a hairbrush for his fur.

Myc'hal Yosef, Kwsk yn Kres

Myc'hal Yosef, kwsk yn kres,
kov kÿweith ker c'hwath ysy dhÿn,
'ma dhâ eskÿrn yn-dan dhoar,
lim ann lagha's loskas tynn;
lovan gÿlmyz 'gevsis, 'sos,
dhÿ dorc'h dhâ vri ha'th enor,
war ann grog kurunyz 'vus
a gas ha' gweuz ann trec'hor:
Pyw 'wra dybri bara syc'h?
Pyw 'wra eva gwin?
Yn gwoez ann werin c'hwath 'ma tan
'wra dÿwi bÿz y'nn fin.

'Ghwrusis vodya'nn byz rÿ skôn,
koedha 'wrus' ty'n-nanz dow lath,
liwa'nn dhoar dhâ woez a'wrug,
pezi dial 'wra êv c'hwath;
'ghermsis uc'hel ha' garma glew
war dhâ henath, warnan oll,
erc'hi bell ma nag ello
dh'aberth a'gan parth dhÿ-goll:
Pyw 'wra dybri bara syc'h?
Pyw 'wra eva gwin?
Yn gwoez ann werin c'hwath 'ma tan
'wra dÿwi bÿz y'nn fin.

War veic'hdeyrnedh ha' tuz-jentil
'ma kÿndoenow anken dhÿn,
a'skullyas tuz 'dreus tiryow pell
ha' ladra yeith, nanz, gwoen, ha' bryn;
a Vyc'hal Yosef pÿrthwc'h kov,
kazor gwiw heb own nâ' skrudh,
gweisyon werin, pÿrthwc'h arvow,
gwainywc'h gwerth y rudhwoez drudh!
Pyw 'wra dybri bara syc'h?
Pyw 'wra eva gwin?
Yn gwoez ann werin c'hwath 'ma tan
'wra dÿwi bÿz y'nn fin.

Michael Joseph, Sleep in Peace

Michael Joseph,[1] sleep in peace, we still remember you as a dear comrade, your bones are under earth, it was the lime of the law that fiercely burned them; it was a knotted rope that you got, boy, as the wreath of your renown and honour, on the gallows you were crowned from the hatred and mockery of the conqueror: *Who will eat dry bread? Who will drink wine? In the blood of the ordinary people there is still fire that will blaze to the end.*

You indeed left the world too quickly, you fell down two yards, your blood coloured the earth, it still prays for vengeance; you shouted loud and shouted boldly to your posterity, to us all, ordering a struggle so that your sacrifice on our behalf will not be lost: *Who will eat dry bread? Who will drink wine? In the blood of the ordinary people there is still fire that will blaze to the end.*

Against kings and nobles we have debts of misery, who scattered people over distant lands and stole language, valley, down and hill; – let us remember Michael Joseph, a worthy warrior without fear or shudder, fellows of the common people, let us bear arms, let us earn the value of his costly red blood: *Who will eat dry bread? Who will drink wine? In the blood of the ordinary people there is still fire that will blaze to the end.*

Ann Gwinlanneug ha'nn Katheuz

Ydh yze gwinlanneug y'nn nanz,
    y'nn nanz,
a'nn zÿvu pymp gwwrgath ha' kanz,
    ha' kanz;
rag dyndyl y arghanz
yn dydhyow y vywnanz
y'kane'nn gwinlanneug ha'nn katheuz:
ha'nn katheuz,
pymp gwwrgath ha' kanz,
pymp gwwrgath ha' kanz,
y'kane'nn gwinlanneug ha'nn katheuz.

Y'kanenz heb hedhi peub nos,
    peub nos,
a'ga esedh yn res war ann fos,
    ann fos;
y'kanenz yn-uc'hel,
y'kanenz yn-isel,
ha' kÿntell mîlvîlyow peub seîthenn,
peub seîthenn,
yn res war ann fos,
yn res war ann fos,
ha' kÿntell mîlvîlyow peub seîthenn.

Mez sowaeth! gwoe vy! Nanz yw pell
    yw pell,
y'tdaethonz dhÿ dhywedh pur fell,
    pur fell;
pan goedhas ann katheuz
ha'nn dyn bÿz y'nn gwoedheuz
ha'ga gwaska dhÿ win rudh brentin:
rudh brentin,
dhÿ dhywedh pur fell,
dhÿ dhywedh pur fell,
ha'ga gwaska dhÿ win rudh brentin.

The Vintner and the Cats

There was a vintner in the valley, *in the valley*, who had a hundred and five tomcats, *a hundred*; to earn his money in the days of his life the vintner would sing with the cats, with the cats, *with the cats, a hundred and five tomcats, a hundred and five tomcats, the vintner would sing with the cats.*

They would sing without ceasing every night, *every night*, sitting in a row on the wall, *the wall*; they would sing high, they would sing low, and collect millions every week, *every week, and collect millions every week, in a row on the wall, in a row on the wall, and collect millions every week*.

But alas, woe is me! A long time ago, *long ago*, they came to a very cruel end, *very cruel*; when the cats and the man fell into the lees and were pressed into a noble red wine: *noble red, to a very cruel end, to a very cruel end, and were pressed into a noble red wine.*

Jevodí[1]

Pan dremmenyth zy kornel ann stret,
my a'festin hag ot! my a'th fvet,
gwort un polz, y'th saluzav yn-tdwr,
jevodí, ro dhâ leuv, par amwr!
Jevodí, 'dhamsel c'hweg, jevodí,
'fvynnav peub pryz dhâ gara dhyzí;
jevodí, 'dhamsel c'hweg, jevodí,
'fvynnav peub pryz dhâ gara dhyzí.

Ganz dhâ vinc'hwardh, ty aeles a'nn Nev,
dhâ jentiles 'dhistewys ow lev,
ty rÿ'strothas ow bryz hyz-ha'-hyz,
jevodí, bÿz yn gworphenn ann byz.
Jevodí, 'dhamsel c'hweg, jevodí,
'fvynnav peub pryz dhâ gara dhyzí;
jevodí, 'dhamsel c'hweg, jevodí,
'fvynnav peub pryz dhâ gara dhyzí.

Dhÿ'nn dywottÿ a-barth dhÿmmo deuz,
ma ydh esedhyn y'nn gornel y'nn skeuz,
tÿrri syc'hez heb lett ni a'vynn,
jevodí, my, nynz ov senzyaz tynn.
Jevodí, 'dhamsel c'hweg, jevodí,
'fvynnav peub pryz dhâ gara dhyzí;
jevodí, 'dhamsel c'hweg, jevodí,
'fvynnav peub pryz dhâ gara dhyzí.

'Fvynnav kana dhâ wormeul ha'th kloz,
hag a-woze dhÿ'w chÿ ni a'roz,
heb dhâ serc'h, 'dhamsel c'hweg, 'fvydhav manz,
jevodí, 'dhamsel c'hweg, torr ow c'hwanz!
Jevodí, 'dhamsel c'hweg, jevodí,
'fvynnav peub pryz dhâ gara dhyzí;
jevodí, 'dhamsel c'hweg, jevodí,
'fvynnav peub pryz dhâ gara dhyzí.

I Tell You[2]

When you pass the corner of the street, I'll hurry and catch up with you, wait a moment, I'll greet you courageously, I tell you, give me your hand for love's sake. *I tell you, sweet maid[3], I tell you, I'll always love you, I tell you, sweet maid, I tell you, I'll always love you.*

With your smile, you angel from Heaven, it's your gentleness that has silenced my voice, it's you who's captured my mind completely, I tell you, till the end of the world. *I tell you, sweet maid, I tell you, I'll always love you, I tell you, sweet maid, I tell you, I'll always love you.*

To the pub come with me, so that we'll sit in a shady corner, we'll quench our thirst with nothing to prevent us, I tell you, I'm not a tight-fisted miser. *I tell you, sweet maid, I tell you, I'll always love you, I tell you, sweet maid, I tell you, I'll always love you.*

I'll sing your praise and your glory, and afterwards to my house we'll stroll. Without your love, sweet maid, I'll be crippled, I tell you, sweet maid, quench my desire. *I tell you, sweet maid, I tell you, I'll always love you, I tell you, sweet maid, I tell you, I'll always love you.*

Lymnores

Y'senz hi hyz ann vre ha'nn prenn;
y'tav hi frenn dowr gwynn worth ann ryz:
gwareg seîthliwyz a'c'hwevr yn hy phenn.

Painter[1]

She grasps the tallness of the hill and the tree;
she touches the excitement of white water at the
ford:
a seven-coloured arch glistens in her head.

Talek

(E.G.R. Hooper)

Ny'daw ann lev, ny'daw ann bardh;
peub dydh a'dardh, ha' peub gwoal, heb grev:
kowst a'rÿ glasnev, peub dagrenn hy c'hwardh.

Talek

(E.G.R. Hooper)[1]

The voice[2] will not fall silent, the poet will not fall silent;
every day will break, and every feast, without distress:
a rainstorm will give blue heaven, every tear its laugh.

Gelvynak

(Richard Gendall)

Neuz geiryow gwir ha' kovow sanz
yn gweow arghanz a-estynn hir
dre havow'nn hendir, mîl leun ha' pymp kanz.

Gelvynak

(Richard Gendall)[1]

Threads of true words and sacred memories
in webs of silver stretching long
a full thousand and a half of the ancient land's
summers.

Ow Thaz

Ha'y dhorn ganz raj ow' tava'nn prenn
y'nadhe'nn wydhenn war alteur staj
yn-pareuz dhÿ drummaj na'dhoe dhÿ-benn.

My Father[1]

With his hand carefully touching the wood
he hewed the tree on the altar of a slipway
reader for a sea voyage that would not come
to an end.

Ann Vamm Nëwydh

Ow' lenwyl lesk y'formyav byz;
dhÿ skorrow gwydhryz y'roav deil fresk:
a vaes ann morresk y'ghwraav porva glyz.

The New Mother

By filling a cradle I shall create a world;
to withered branches I shall give fresh leaves:
from the open land of the sea marsh I shall
make fertile pasture.

Baner ann Werin

Dre gneuz ann prowt y'rez mîl skrudh
pan wel, yn kÿstudh, ann renkow stowt,
pan gryn rag owndhowt a'nn vaner splann rudh.

The People's Flag

Through the flesh of the arrogant will run a thousand shudders
when, in confusion, he sees the steadfast ranks,
and quivers in fear of the bright red flag.

Dorn ann Oberydh

Skwith kyn y'fvydh a lieus pryz,
c'hwath y'gan bryz del wythyn ann fydh,
dorn ann oberydh rÿ'wonydhas byz.

The Hand of the Worker

Although at many times it is tired,
still in our minds we keep the faith,
that it is the hand of the worker that has
wrought a world.

Dowr Byc'han

Ann gwolow glan yn froz lymm gro;
rennyn yn ro lyrow brath ann tan:
amm ann dowr byc'han a'wra dhÿmm ann tro.

Little Water[1]

The clear light in a sharp fresh stream;
let us share as a gift liquids with the bite of the
fire:
it is the kiss of the little water that will suffice
for me.

Saoirse

(4/vii/98)

Yn-rag, yn-bann, niz, pon, ha lamm,
ro byrl hag amm dhÿ'nn gwolow fraeth splann
loerwynz ha' stergann ow' lentri y'th kâmm.

Saoirse[1]

(4/vii/98)[2]

Onwards, upwards, fly, run, and leap,
give an embrace and a kiss to the fluid
bright light
while the moon's wind and the starlight
gleam in your step.

Tremmenanz

Y'fes ann gwynz ann deil a'nn gwydh;
Ny'dheu dhÿ-nes a hyz oll y hynz:
ann amser rakkynz a'dec'h rag a'vydh.

Passing

The wind will chase the leaves from the trees;
it will come no closer the whole length of its path:
the former time will retreat from that which is to be.

Kaer Dherw

A-vaes a'nn mur y'seiv bryn glas;
ann lanwez vas a'dhÿc'hwel yn-sur:
un lagaz gwelbur na'c'hwil ÿna plas.

Derry[1]

Outside the wall there stands a green hill;
the shallow tide will surely return:
there is one pure-seeing eye that will not seek there a habitation.

Hikka Trev Vedhyg

(Devisyor ann tanvarc'h)

Ann hoarn ha'nn tan a'dhÿnyth toth
yn kreuth vaen koth dre nerth ann daran,
ha'nn kledhrow a'gan serc'h bellder del gôth.

Richard Trevithick

(The inventor of the steam locomotive)

It is the iron and the fire that will beget speed
in the womb of old stone through the strength of the thunder,
and the rails that will sing fitting love of distance.

Dhÿ-vaes

Dhÿ-vaes y'kerdhsis a-hyz fordh galez,
ha'nn luzw owth yeina war ann oelez,
dhÿ-vaes y'kerdhsis bÿz y'nn tywlgow,
y'nn nos ma y'th ghworris vy a-gynzow.

Bÿz y'nn tywlezyon my a'th ghworras,
dagrow poes y'th tdowlagaz downlas,
eryanz y'th lev ha' sorr y'th kolonn,
ha'nn nos owth enkleudhyaz pellarm mordonn.

A'nn gworwel down y'tardh dydh nëwydh,
deil a'goedh a skorr skwith ann derwwydh,
bledhenn yn oes a'sew peub bledhenn,
ha'nn nos 'mma a'dÿwl hy skeuz diworphenn.

Away

Away you walked along a hard road,
while the ash grew cold on the hearth,
away you walked into the obscurity, in
the night where I put you not long ago.

Into that darkness I put you, heavy tears
in your deep blue eyes, defiance in your
voice and anger in your heart, as the
night buried the distant cry of a sea-
wave.

From the deep horizon will break a new
day, leaves will fall from the tired
branches of the oak trees, a year in an
age will follow every year, and this night
will throw its unfinishing shadow.

An Dhyw Wisk

Y'ghweav byz a bedeir elvenn,
kewni, glaswelz, loen ha' gwydhenn;
y'n liwav dhÿz a dhowr ann feunteun,
lew ha' lowarn, logeuz, meuryeun:
ann tir ha'nn mor, ann aer ha'nn tan,
levow, flammow, meyn ha' holan.

Ha' my a'we ow byz a wythi,
larjes, lagha, menestrothi;
a woez y'fvyskav liwyow lawer,
mo ha' mitin kler, gworthewer:
ann oes ha'nn polz, ann eur ha'nn mis,
teyrnyon, tornow, henis, enis.

Y'troc'hav gwisk a'nn bras ha'nn byc'han,
bryn, brialli, stergann, tredan,
a dhuder nos y'ghwriav ammal,
hun ann loer, kwsk spus ann aval:
ann tir ha'nn mor, ann aer ha'nn tan,
levow, flammow, meyn ha' holan.

Ha' my a'drÿc'h ow gwisk a gÿher,
gwobern, tresor, jorneth, euryer;
hy ammal my a's gwra a'nn nosweîth,
gwow ha' glori, kamm ha' perfeith:
ann oes ha'nn polz, ann eur ha'nn mis,
teyrnyon, tornow, henis, enis.

Y'ghwriav nerth ann Noar y'm kerc'hynn,
mor ha' lagenn, mÿnydh, tywynn;
y'm gwisk y'kerdhav maes ann meuredh,
lefeinz,lughez, hinon, tewedh:
ann tir ha'nn mor, ann aer ha'nn tan,
levow, flammow, meyn ha' holan.

Y'm kerc'hynn vy y'ghwiskav hiraeth,
serc'h ha' bysow, bedhvaen, moraeth;
yn maes ann golonn leun y'kerdhav,
lent ha' jolyv, skôn hag arav:
ann oes ha'nn polz, ann eur ha'nn mis,
teyrnyon, tornow, henis, enis.

The Two Costumes

I shall weave a world from four elements, moss, green grass, bush and tree; I shall colour it for you with the water of the spring, lion and fox, mice, ants: *the land and the sea, the air and the fire, voices, flames, stones and salt.*

And it is I who shall weave my world from veins, generosity, law, instrumental music; with blood I shall mix many colours, small hours and bright morning, evening: *the age and the moment, the hour and the month, government ministers, workshifts, ancient custom, aniseed.*

I shall cut a costume from the big and the small, hill, primroses, starlight, electricity; with the blackness of night I shall sew a hem, the falling asleep of the moon, the sleep of the pips of the apple: *the land and the sea, the air and the fire, voices, flames, stones and salt.*

And it is I who shall cut my costume with muscle, wages, treasure, working day, working hours; its edge I shall make from the nighttime, falsehood and splendour, bent and perfect: *the age and the moment, the hour and the month, government ministers, workshifts, ancient custom, aniseed.*

I shall sew the strength of the Earth about me, sea and puddle, mountain, dune; in my costume I shall walk the field of majesty, frogs, lightning, good weather, bad weather: *the land and the sea, the air and the fire, voices, flames, stones and salt.*

About me I shall put on longing, love and a ring, gravestone, mourning, in the field of the full heart I shall walk, slow-witted and lively, quick and slow-moving: *the age and the moment, the hour and the month, government ministers, workshifts, ancient custom, aniseed.*

Ny'woer Flÿc'hez Nivera Mann

Ny'woer flÿc'hez nivera mann
euryow'nn dydh nâ' phoesow'nn loergann;
ny'woedhonz hyz nâ' lez ann byz
nâ' niver ann spassow kÿllyz
yn-maes a dhrehaedh peub a'c'hwer,
yn-maes a dhanjer ann niver.

Ny'dheur floc'h vyth a hoedhl ann dydh
nâ' genyzygaeth ann mÿnydh;
ny'verkyonz p'eur y'fveirw ann nos
woze anwelder ann gwortos
yn-maes a dhrehaedh peub a'c'hwer,
yn-maes a dhanjer ann niver.

A-vodh dhÿ riv hanw ny'n roonz;
kÿppár hag asynn war garrbonz
y'tdrailyons onen, deg po kanz
yn-maes a diredh dÿsmygyanz
yn-maes a dhrehaedh peub a'c'hwer,
yn-maes a dhanjer ann niver.

Yn-fveur y'senz floc'h hudhow, mez
heb tryzedh, degvez nâ c'hanzvez;
ny'niver, marz oel nerth y benn,
ann gynzza nâ'nn vîlvez dagrenn
yn-maes a dhrehaedh peub a'c'hwer,
yn-maes a dhanjer ann niver.

Children Do Not Know How to Count at All

Children do not know how to count at all the hours of the day or the weight of the moonlight; they do not know the length or breadth of the world or the number of lost opportunities *out of the reach of everything that grieves, out of the jurisdiction of the number.*

No child at all cares about the lifespan of the day or the birth of the mountain; they do not take note of when the night dies after the invisibility of the waiting *out of the reach of everything that grieves, out of the jurisdiction of the number.*

It is not willingly that to a number they will give a name; like a donkey on a cart-bridge they will drag one, ten or hundred out of the territory of the act of imagining *out of the reach of everything that grieves, out of the jurisdiction of the number.*

It is greatly that a child will esteem outbursts of merriment, but without third, tenth or hundredth; it will not count, if it weeps with all its strength, the first or the thousandth tear *out of the reach of everything that grieves, out of the jurisdiction of the number.*

Dyski ann Rivow

Pan dhyskyth rezyaz ann rivow,
y'tdyskyth dewis gwir po gwow.

Pymp a'gar onen a golonn leun:
bydh c'hwec'hez yn mysk ann pymp, c'hwec'hez!
Pezwar a'bon a-rag deinzow keun:
bydh pympez y'ga mysk, bydh pympez!

Pan dhyskyth rezyaz ann rivow,
y'tdyskyth dewis gwir po gwow.

Tri a'gan heb gwersyow dhÿ'ga thon:
bydh pezwaredh, 'sos, bydh pezwaredh!
Dow a'rann kwartron torth a lawn skôn:
bydh tryzedh, tryzedh, tryzedh, tryzedh!

Pan dhyskyth rezyaz ann rivow,
y'tdyskyth dewis gwir po gwow.

Onen a'seiv yn ammal ann skeuz:
hebdho fattel niveryth, fattel?
Pyw a'th kÿmmer yntre bys ha' meuz?
Py glem a'worthworryth dh'y gwarel?

Pan dhyskyth rezyaz ann rivow,
y'tdyskyth dewis gwir po gwow.

Learning the Numbers

When you learn the rhythm of the numbers, you will learn to choose truth or falsehood.

It is five who will love one of a full heart: be sixth amongst the five, sixth. It is four who will run before the teeth of dogs: be fifth amongst them, be fifth.

When you learn the rhythm of the numbers, you will learn to choose truth or falsehood.

It is three who will sing without verses to their tune: be fourth, boy, be fourth. It is two who will divide a quarter of a loaf with a quick blade: be third, third, third, third.

When you learn the rhythm of the numbers, you will learn to choose truth or falsehood.

It is one who will stand in the edge of the shadow: without him how will you count, how? Who will take you between finger and thumb? What defence will you raise to his claim?

When you learn the rhythm of the numbers, you will learn to choose truth or falsehood.

Ann Gwydr-Miraz

Dhÿmm y'kÿmmunas kynz ow mamm-wynn
gwydr-miraz ha' starn yn-kerc'hynn,
hirgylc'h gravbrenn yn-faedhus ha' poes,
kÿppár ha' gwareg yn hen egloes:
a'w mamm-wynn hagen ny'm bu kov glan
pan varwse hi ha' my c'hwath baban;
fysk y'm bysyez, y'm kolonn vy baz
owth egÿri ann fardell wastaz:
Mir ha' preder, preder ha' mir,
gwelez ann gwow, gwelez ann gwir!

P'rag y'ghwruig yvel, c'hwath mann ny'woen,
un dywedh-dydh brav ha' my moroen,
dÿsedha'nn gwydr-miraz a y sav
y'nn gëgin vras yn gwolow'nn Kynyav;
a-rag ann gwydr ydh esedhis polz
ha' frea a y fun ow melynnwolz,
miraz ganz mall bÿz y'nn hirboll huz
ma y'fveudhsoz peub esow ha' gwoluz:
Mir ha' preder, preder ha' mir,
gwelez ann gwow, gwelez ann gwir!

Y'ghwelis minc'hwardh mawes dheg bloedh
ha'y gwolz ow' froza bÿz dh'y dywskoedh,
tywl hy dowlagaz, dywrudh ganz tan,
leun hy byz a beub gwolow didhan;
stevell yn-ghwlyc'hyz ganz ec'hwedh c'hwar
a howlwynn a'wolc'he peub galar;
dre'nn fenestr agor, roth nanz ha' bryn
yn-rewyz y'nn pellderow ylyn:
Mir ha' preder, preder ha' mir,
gwelez ann gwow, gwelez ann gwir!

Pan assaiis tava hy c'hneuz fîn,
yeinder y'n drehaedhas ow ewin:
yn le'nn vawessig ydh yze ben
rÿ'dhifunse dhÿ vitin Gweinten
yn-bann yn-un worra hy gwolz du
yn torc'hennow kÿmpenn a-dhowdu,
ha'y eneb yrdeg yn-fvyw a frenn
avél tesawel dre yz gwresenn:
Mir ha' preder, preder ha' mir,
gwelez ann gwow, gwelez ann gwir!

The Looking Glass

To me my grandmother left a long time ago a looking glass surrounded by a frame, an oval of carved wood, ornately beautiful and heavy, like an arch in an ancient church: now, of my grandmother I had no clear memory, since she had died while I was still a baby; with haste in my fingers, stupefaction in my heart at opening the flat parcel: *Look and think, think and look, see the lie, see the truth.*

Why I did thus, still by no means I know, one afternoon when I was a young girl, arranging the looking glass standing in the big kitchen in the light of the Autumn; before the glass I sat for a moment and released from its band my yellow hair, looked eagerly into the long magic pool where all dearth and opulence were drowned: *Look and think, think and look, see the lie, see the truth.*

I saw the smile of a girl of ten years with her hair flowing down to her shoulders, dark her eyes, cheeks afire, her world full of every pleasing light, room drenched by a mild late afternoon with sunlight that washed away every pain; through the open window, the shape of a valley and a hill frozen in the transparent distances: *Look and think, think and look, see the lie, see the truth.*

When I tried to touch her fine flesh, it was coldness that my nail reached; instead of the little girl there was a maiden who had awoken on a Spring morning putting up her black hair in neat coils on either side, and her fresh fair face alive with excitement like a sultry breeze through corn in fertile ground: *Look and think, think and look, see the lie, see the truth.*

Y'kilyas ann ven yn-dan ow bys,
y'teudhas mel ann howlwynn melys
hag yn-tromm ydh yze loergann yein
ow' fenna bÿz y'nn hirgylc'h stanzvein;
yn-maes a'nn downder y'selle'n-leith
dowlagaz na'gwskse teir nosweîth,
ganow skwith a'furvye minc'hwardh kromm,
askre a'wythe floc'h dhÿ wodomm:
Mir ha' preder, preder ha' mir,
gwelez ann gwow, gwelez ann gwir!

War ann gwydr ydh anedhlis yn-lent
heb surnedh y'm kolonn a'm entent,
hag ydh ÿmmlezas ann nywl yn-skôn
a-dreus ann lyvneneb mar dhison;
y'neuvyas bezeth nëwydh dhÿ'w gwel
yn-un dhoen amserolow kruel,
skeuz yn kneuz ann dhywrudh ha' dhÿ'w baz,
pluv tywl worth kornelow'nn dhowlagaz:
Mir ha' preder, preder ha' mir,
gwelez ann gwow, gwelez ann gwir!

Skrudh a'sugere yn-nanz ow c'hein,
dre'w c'holonn y'froze gwoez poesyein,
mez ot ann eneb dhÿ fin un dydh
ow' newiz y fysmant a-nëwydh,
ann ganow dhÿ voan, ann gwolz dhÿ wynn,
loeznedh gworthewer Gwav y'nn tremmynn!
Mez y'pevre'nn dhowlagaz heb eudh,
kÿppár ha' pollow yn hen vaengleudh:
Mir ha' preder, preder ha' mir,
gwelez ann gwow, gwelez ann gwir!

A-dreus ow thal y'tynnis leuv skav,
dÿglena ow skubwolz liw kalav;
a'nn pyth a'welyn y'pÿrthis own
ow' miraz y'nn pÿllynn kalettown,
mez c'hwath y'fvinc'hwardhe eneb kryc'h,
dowlagaz a-neuv yn fass bloedhsyc'h,
kroghen disliw, dywrudh gow, gwolz kann,
c'hwath tan war ann oelez regythwann:
Mir ha' preder, preder ha' mir,
gwelez ann gwow, gwelez ann gwir!

Pan dhalghennis y'nn gammeug ganz mall,
miraz dre wydr dhÿ'nn byz arall,
selloz ha' selloz a'm yeunez leun
kÿppár ha' c'hwythra gwoelez feunteun,

The maiden receded under my finger, the honey of the sweet sunshine melted and suddenly cold moonlight was overflowing into the hermetically-sealed oval; out of the depth moistly gazed a pair of eyes that had not slept for three nights, a tired mouth that formed a curved smile, a bosom that kept a child warm: *Look and think, think and look, see the lie, see the truth.*

On the glass I breathed slowly without any certainty as to my intent in my heart, and the mist spread quickly across the smooth surface so soundlessly and quickly; a new face swam to my sight bearing cruel traces of time, a shadow in the flesh of the cheeks and, to my stupefaction, dark feathers at the corners of the eyes: *Look and think, think and look, see the lie, see the truth.*

It was a shudder that trickled down my back, through my heart that ran heavy cold blood, but here was the face at the end of a certain day changing its appearance once again, the mouth thin, the hair white, greyness of a winter evening in the expression. But the eyes shone without terror, like pools in an old quarry: *Look and think, think and look, see the lie, see the truth.*

Across my forehead I drew a light hand, shook my sweeping straw-coloured hair; of what I had seen I was afraid, from looking into the hard deep rock pool, but still the wrinkled face smiled, a pair of eyes afloat in a face dried by years of life, pale skin, hollow cheeks, pure-white hair, fire yet on the ember-weak hearth: *Look and think, think and look, see the lie, see the truth*.

When I grasped the rim eagerly, looked through glass to the other world, gazed and gazed with my full longing, I saw a

y'ghwelis kroglenn a-niz y'nn nos,
fenestr avlavar yn-dan wortos
leuv na's dÿgaee, heb marz vyth oll,
haneth, nâ' bÿz dydh joi po argoll:
Mir ha' preder, preder ha' mir,
gwelez ann gwow, gwelez ann gwir!

Ÿna ow' miraz ydh yzen vy
worth teudhanz avél ergh warleny,
peub liw, peub roth yn-dan froza'n-fraeth
yn lonklynn lentrus avél galaeth
ha' gaza a-woze spavenn sanz
c'hwevreneb disÿmmuz lynn arghanz,
bÿz ma y'ghwelis dhÿ'nn polz 'na heb ken,
fêst yn-tromm, ow eneb ow honen:
Mir ha' preder, preder ha' mir,
gwelez ann gwow, gwelez ann gwir!

Ledan ha' leith ow dowlagaz glas
yn-leun a c'hwilgaranz ha' mysmas
woze gwelez dre'nn hirgylc'h mar gler
bÿz yn hunroz vezethow lawer;
a-dreiv dhÿmm y'roas ann darraz kleb
ma y'nizas ow dywleuv dhÿ'm eneb,
hag ot ow mamm, ganz gwynz yn hy dorn,
prenazow hy c'hanstell yn tasorn!
Mir ha' preder, preder ha' mir,
gwelez ann gwow, gwelez ann gwir!

curtain in flight in the night, a mute window waiting for a hand that would not close it, beyond any doubt, tonight, or until the day of joy or perdition: *Look and think, think and look, see the lie, see the truth.*

Then I was looking at a melting like last year's snow, every colour, every shape flowing fluently in a shining whirlpool like a galaxy and leaving afterwards a holy lull of the motionless shining surface of the lake of silver, so that I saw, only that moment, very suddenly my own face: *Look and think, think and look, see the lie, see the truth.*

Broad and blue my two blue eyes full of curiosity and bewilderment after seeing through the oval so bright into a dream of many faces; behind me the door gave a slam so that my hands flew to my face, and here was my mother, out of breath, shopping piled up in her basket: *Look and think, think and look, see the lie, see the truth.*

Edreg

A' c'hwegenn bell, â kwoedhyes
a'rÿyn rag dhâ dhrÿi dhÿ-nes,
rag teudha maes ha' mîldir,
dÿgaea evander tir,
war-barth y'reknes niver
ann tyweuz ha'nn gwelz ha'nn ster
mez fellyl c'hwath rÿi musur
dhÿ veinz ow edreganz pur.

A' c'hwegenn drist, â kallen
dÿc'hwelez un polz heb ken
dhÿ bryzweîth drÿc'hi kolonn
avél tÿrri ewynn donn,
a'th kneuz y'tynnen galar,
gwoe a'th tdowlagaz heb par,
gwiska a'th parth peub kadoen,
y'th le zy pÿrthi peub poen.

 pen, â c'hwegenn gÿllyz,
war uc'helse gwynn ann byz,
ann oesow pell y'm danjer,
skianz ha' galloz y'm mer,
y'losken drein ha' krinc'hwynn,
tynna amser a y wreidh tynn,
planza haz nëwydh bywnanz
yn hen weryz chonz ha' c'hwanz.

Regret

Oh distant sweet one, if you knew what I would give in order to bring you nearer, in order to melt field and mile, close breadth of land, together you would add the number of the sand and the grass and the stars but still be unable to give measure to the amount of my utter repentance.

Oh sad sweet one, if I could return only one moment to the instant of the breaking of a heart like the breaking of the foam of a wave, from your flesh I should draw pain, and woe from your matchless eyes, wear for your sake every chain, in your stead bear every pain.

If I were, oh lost sweet one, on the bright high throne of the world, the long ages in my jurisdiction, knowledge and power in my marrow, I should burn thorns and shrivelled weeds, pull up time from its taut roots, plant the seeds of new life in the ancient soil of chance and desire.

Ni

A nebeuz hal y'trÿc'hyn ann maes,
kaea parkow a'nn tiredh anaes,
gwonyz gwoenow gwylz dhÿ wresenn c'hweg,
bugeilya deveiz, gwytha gwartheg.
Y'n panz war ann ros 'mma y'splann poll stronk
pan sudh liw'nn ebrenn yn y islonk,
treilya dowr mostyyz dhÿ lyr mar lan,
yn-frank a vlas peub leiz po holan.
Pan settyyn dalgenn yn doar ha' tir,
dhÿn y'fvydh leilder, dhÿn y'fvydh gwir,
y'nn erwi trenk, ydh egÿryn ar,
gwolc'hi'nn gweryz a geudh ha' galar.
Y'kÿll ann eur hy danjer ha'y soedh
pan bawes dhâ benn polz war ow skoedh,
ha' dorn pan y'n settyn polz yn dorn,
gwoez a'gan y'nn kneuz, mer y'nn askorn.

A nebeuz meyn y'tdrec'hevyn din
war warthev ann vre kynz ez mitin,
dhÿ vur ow' treilya kerrygi karn,
a atl ow' trec'hevyl twr kadarn.
Y'seiv ann ammug worth gwynzow feuz,
dhÿ neb a'n mynno profya gwoskeuz,
hag omma y'trov gwandryaz y drev
yn kylc'h kaeryz kow war ann gwarthev.
Pan fwndyyn annedh yn din ha' twr,
ni a'vydh stowt ha' ni a'vydh dwr,
y'nn bewdern statli y'senzyn gwledh,
lenwyl moes a laz ha' lawenedh.
Y'kÿll ann eur hy danjer ha'y soedh
pan bawes dhâ benn polz war ow skoedh,
ha' moes pan y'n lezyn ni y'nn hel,
y'c'hwav ann c'hwerththin c'hwar dh'enawel,

A nebeuz kÿnuz y'teinyn tan
a'leinw kwrrow'nn oelez evan,
hÿrdhya lanwezow gwolow ha' gwres
dhÿ veudhi'nn tywlezyon dibawes.
War ann oelez 'mma y'ghenyr dydh
ha'nn loer c'hwath ow' kana dh'y c'hwëyrydh,
y'plenzyr haz ann howl y'nn du down,
gwonyz gwreidh Paradhys yn Annown.
Pan drovyyn solas yn c'hwavow tes,
ni a'geiv c'hwarder, ni a'geiv les,

We

From a little moorland we shall hew the open ground, enclose the difficult territory into fields, cultivate wild downs into sweet fertile ground, herd sheep, keep cattle. In a hollow on this heath a polluted pool will shine when the colour of the sky sinks into its abyss, turning dirty water to a liquid so clear, free from the taste of all mud or salt. When we take possession of the land, ours will be faithfulness, ours will be truth, in the sour acres we shall open tilth, wash from the soil anguish and pain. *The hour will lose its jurisdiction and its office when your head rests for a moment on my shoulder,* and when we place hand for a moment on hand, blood will sing in the flesh, marrow in the bone.

From a few stones we shall build a fortress on the summit of the hill before morning, turning the rocks of a cairn into a wall, from rubble building a mighty tower. The defences will withstand the winds of fate, to whoever wishes offering shelter, and it is here that a wanderer shall find his home in a hollow fortified circle on the summit. When we establish a habitation in fortress and tower, it is we who shall be steadfast, we who shall be courageous, in the magnificent refectory we shall hold a feast, fill a table with drink and joy. *The hour will lose its jurisdiction and its office when your head rests for a moment on my shoulder,* and when we set a table in the hall, the gentle laughter will swell into a storm.

From a little fuel we shall kindle a fire that will fill the limits of the broad hearth, send out tides of light and warmth to drown the unresting darkness. On this hearth a day will be born even while the moon is still singing to her sisters, the seed of the sun will be planted in the deep black, cultivating the roots of Paradise in Hades. When we find

haza hav byc'han yn straz ann Gwav,
lannerc'h ma y'tÿv howlsudhow arav.
Y'kÿll ann eur hy danjer ha'y soedh
pan bawes dhâ benn polz war ow skoedh,
ha' peir pan y's gwolc'hyn yn froz dan,
dhÿ vîl ydh haedhyn sosten maglan.

A nebeuz bleuz y'pÿbyn torth domm
rag tÿrri nown gworthewer glawlomm,
dhÿ wres ha' kneuz ow' treilya dowst gwynn,
holya'nn burumm dre'nn toes pan eskynn.
War ann bara 'mma y'teudh ann mel
yn-tdrÿyz a dhilyow downna'nn gworwel,
ha' bÿz y'nn gwythi pan goedh ann peill
y'porthav kov a'nn havow ereill.
Pan drovyyn sosten yn c'hwydh ann toes,
dhÿn y'fvydh bywnanz, dhÿn y'fvydh oes,
maga'nn flÿc'hez wywyz aga lev,
aga lenwyl a gan ann hendrev.
Y'kÿll ann eur hy danjer ha'y soedh
pan bawes dhâ benn polz war ow skoedh,
ha' peub degh hag avorow kÿphrýz
a'ÿmmvet y'th hedhyw difunyz.

pleasure in gusts of warmth, it is we who shall find gentleness, we who shall find benefit, seeding a little summer in the valley bottom of winter, a clearing where slow sunsets will grow. *The hour will lose its jurisdiction and its office when your head rests for a moment on my shoulder,* and when we wash a cauldron in a stream of fire, to a thousand we shall serve wholesome nourishment.

From a little flour we shall bake a warm loaf to satisfy the hunger of a rainswept afternoon, into warmth and flesh turning white dust, following the yeast when it rises through the dough. On this bread the honey will melt, brought from the deepest petals of the horizon, and when the pollen falls when the pollen falls into the veins I shall remember the other summers. When we find nourishment in the swell of the dough, ours will be life, ours will be an age, feeding the children of the withered voices, filling them with the song of the homestead. *The hour will lose its jurisdiction and its office when your head rests for a moment on my shoulder,* and every day and tomorrow also will meet in your woken today.

P'ann dra 'leveryn dhÿdhi?

Dhÿdhi p'ann dra 'leveryn?
(Gwag ann stret, loergann war vryn.)
Ydh yw hi ow c'hÿweithes
(senz vy'n-tener, gwask vy'n-nes!)
P'ann dra 'leveryn dhÿdhi–
gwow byc'han c'hwath, dow po tri?
P'ann dra 'leveryn dhÿdhi?
Dhÿdhi p'ann dra 'leveryn?

Dhÿdhi p'ann dra 'leveryn?
(Karr dre'nn stret, gwynz yein war vryn.)
Rÿ'vu hi ow c'hÿweithes
(nynz oelav– p'ann dra yw'nn les?)
P'ann dra 'leveryn dhÿdhi?
Martesen, rÿ'glywas si.
P'ann dra 'leveryn dhÿdhi?
Dhÿdhi p'ann dra 'leveryn?

Dhÿdhi p'ann dra 'leveryn?
(Trëyz y'nn stret, howlwynn war vryn.)
Ydh o hi ow c'hÿweithes
(hedh ganz stlevi– gaz dhÿmm kres!)
P'ann dra 'leveryn dhÿdhi?
Fattel wortheb? Taw po kri?
P'ann dra 'leveryn dhÿdhi?
Dhÿdhi p'ann dra 'leveryn?

What Are We Going to Tell Her?

What are we going to tell her? (The street empty, moonlight on a hill.) She is my friend (hold me gently, hold me closer!) What shall we tell her – another little lie, two or three? *What shall we tell her? What are we going to tell her?*

What are we going to tell her? (Car through the street, cold wind on a hill.) She has been my friend (I'm not going to cry – what will be the good?) What shall we tell her? Perhaps she's heard a rumour. *What shall we tell her? What are we going to tell her?*

What are we going to tell her? (Feet in the street, sunlight on a hill.) She was my friend (stop stammering, leave me alone!) What shall we tell her? How will she answer? In silence or by crying out? *What shall we tell her? What are we going to tell her?*

Hav Kÿllyz

Sawor lweredh,
 blas aer las;
ebrenn dhiwdhywedh,
 dydh na'hedh:
kryc'how mynoc'h
war ann morloc'h,
skeuzow ec'hwedh
 war dhowr bas.

Awel voan ac'has,
 gwelz war gnoc'h;
gwynz dhÿz rÿz ammas
 sal y vlas:
gwibyow gwennol,
skethow kommol,
gworwel krÿnnvras,
 kolonn droc'h.

Lammow ann morvoc'h,
 hynz heb ol;
dagrow war dhywvoc'h
 prêst a'm hol:
kri floc'holedh,
koll koseledh,
kovow kreboc'h,
 dowr yn dol.

Keurgan ha' karol,
 gwin ha' medh;
donzya yn trëyzol,
 maen ha' bedh:
deilyow kringras,
moraeth lymmgas,
hiraeth bennfol
 drenk hy blas.

C'hwavennow karenzedh,
joi c'hwath bludhlas,
azgovanz down ha' koc'h,
ponn yn forl fol.

Lost Summer

Smell of the Atlantic, taste of blue air;
endless sky, a day that will not cease:
frequent ripples on the sealake, shad-
ows of late afternoon on shallow water.

Thin keen breeze, grass on a hillock;
salty-tasted wind that has kissed you:
swoops of swallow, strips of cloud,
great round horizon, broken heart.

Dolphins leaping, path without a trace;
tears on cheeks that will constantly
follow me: cry of children, loss of quiet-
ness, shrivelled memories, water in
riverside meadow.

Chorus and carol, wine and mead;
dancing in footprints, stone and grave;
brittle shrivelled leaves, hatefully sharp
morning, mad longing with a sour taste.

Tiny gusts of love, delight still soft and
green, deep and ruddy recollection,
light dust in foolish whirl.

Elynor

Nynz aeth marnaz ann un verc'h
a'nn bedeir dhÿ goll traserc'h
owth eva tynn dyweuz huz
druththa ez owr po gwoluz
dywedh-dydh tomm yn skeuz gwoel
yntre dywlann garregvoel:
growedh rybov, klun worth klun!
Pez kan a'dal ann gurun?

A-dreus ann reverthi glas
kan dorrkolonn y's kanas,
gwe gwersyow galarow glan
Esylz owrwolz ha' Trystan,
dywwydhenn war-barth a-dov,
bwrdhen ow' fetha ankov:
growedh rybov y'th ghwres tont!
Kneuz a'dal pymtheg besont.

War-yow y'froz Avon Rôs
heb hokkya polz nâ' gwortos
yn-un dhrÿi dassonow vyrdh
yn mysk tonnigow donzwyrdh,
hoedhlow leun a lesk dhÿ vedh
yn-dan nennlenn un ec'hwedh:
growedh rybov, kneuz worth kneuz,
gwynn kroghen, du ann gwoskeuz!

Eleanor[1]

Only one daughter of the four was lost to infatuation by drinking a draught of magic drink more precious than gold or riches one warm afternoon in the shadow of a sail between two bald-rocked banks[2]: *lie by my side, hip by hip. How many songs is the crown worth?*

Over the blue flood she sang a song of heartbreak, a web of verses of the pure pain of Isolde of the golden hair and Tristan, two trees growing together, a refrain defeating oblivion: *lie by my side in your impudent warmth. Flesh is worth fifteen bezants.*[3]

Onwards will flow the River Rhône without hesitating or waiting, bringing ten thousand echoes amongst green-dancing little waves, full lifetimes from cradle to grave under the canopy of a single afternoon: *lie by my side, flesh to flesh, white skin, black the shade.*

Daslev

Mez dhâ lev pan dhÿc'hwel,
arta my a'geiv klywez
fattel o frappyow ann tonnow
er bynn ann mur pÿdryz.
Ty a'vynn nivera lieus tan
war vannow mÿnydhyow:
martesen, y'tdyskyth riva
deil ann flammow,
lemen gwell y'fvydh gennyz
gwolc'hi dhâ dhywdroez
war wir rynnell ann gwover.

Echo

But when your voice returns, again I may hear how were the blows of the waves against the rotten wall. It is you who shall count many fires on the tops of mountains: perhaps, you will learn to enumerate the leaves of the flames, but nevertheless you will prefer to wash your feet on the true bed of the brook.

Merwyl a'th Parth

(Noswoal ann Saboth, Londres Gledh)

Merwyl a'th parth ny'vynnav,
a' venen wolz liw kalav,
lemen bywa dydh ha' dydh
poen yr ganz peub howl nëwydh.

Ny'dorrav mann ow syc'hez
owth eva bÿz y'nn gwoelez
gwin kloar ha' fraeth ha' kler ha' fel
a hanaf ganow medhel.

Dhÿ'nn bedh ny'dhieskynnav
rag blas dhâ amm mar arav,
lemen troezya hynzi'nn byz
heb trovya gwoskeuz sawglyz.

Ny'wainyav gwres yn oesow
a'nn frozow gwynnwyrdh gwolow
a'm beudh yn livow soen ha' baz
a dhowloc'h dhâ dhowlagaz.

Merwyl a'th parth ny'vynnen,
gwell bywa'n-kuv ha' lawen,
gwres kneuz dhâ leuv dre'w leuv bÿz mer,
ha' ni a-hynz bÿz pellder.

To Die for your Sake

(The Sabbath Eve, North London)

It is not dying for your sake that I would be, woman of the straw-coloured hair, but rather living day by day fresh pain with each new sun.

I shall not quench my thirst at all by drinking to the bottom cool and swift-flowing and bright and cunning wine from the cup of a soft mouth.

To the grave I shall not descend for the sake of your so-slow kiss, but rather tread the ways of the world without finding any safe warm shelter.

I shall not win any warmth in all eternity from the light green streams of light that will drown me in floods of enchantment and stupefaction from the two lakes of your two eyes.

It is not dying for your part that I would be, better to live kindly and happily, the warmth of your hand through my hand right to the marrow, and us on our way into the distance.

Bara ha' Gwin

Ydhn a'sÿn aga c'hÿzgan
ha' lestri degh a'vydh glan,
peub liw yn-yr ha' nëwydh,
ha'nn nos ow' fÿya a'nn dydh;
ankÿvyn droell, keudh ha' gloes
a'gan esedh worth kÿvoes,
yn-un wonyz grass heb ken
ow' ranna benneuth sosten:
niveryn polzow heb fin,
rennyn torth, dÿnewyn gwin!

Dhÿ bann kanz liw mallarnvrav
y'ghweyn ann minc'hwardh ha'nn tav,
trÿc'hi lennow rag teispann
ma y'ghwriyn a owrneuz splann;
niveryn elvennow vîl,
lawenedh down ha'y beril,
war-barth enawi ann flamm
a'dhonz ganz peub kolonnlamm:
niveryn polzow heb fin,
rennyn torth, dÿnewyn gwin!

A-dhibarth a'gan anvodh
prêst y'fvydhyn a'gan bodh;
hebon ny'vydhyn jammes,
nos a'rÿ dydh, yeinder gwres;
ha'gan trëyz a-hynz dhÿ'nn lann
a'ragsÿn Sul, Gwoal, Kalann,
pan ÿmmblygyyn yn taw meur
war-barth a-rag ann alteur:
niveryn polzow heb fin,
rennyn torth, dÿnewyn gwin!

Bread and Wine

Birds will sound their chorus and yesterday's vessels will be clean, every colour fresh and new, and the night fleeing from the day; let us forget disappointment, travail and anguish as we sit together, only giving thanks by sharing the blessing of nourishment: *let us count moments without limit, let us share a loaf, let us pour wine.*

To a delicate brave cloth of a hundred colours we shall weave the smile and the touch, cut lengths of cloth for a tapestry where we shall sew with golden thread; let us count a thousand elements, deep joy and its danger, together ignite the flame that will dance with every heartbeat: *let us count moments without limit, let us share a loaf, let us pour wine.*

We are constantly willing to be unwilling to be apart; without one another we never are, night gives day and cold, warmth; and it is our feet on the path to the sacred enclosure that will ring in Sunday, Feast Day and First Day when we bow down in great silence together before the altar: *let us count moments without limit, let us share a loaf, let us pour wine.*

Tan Nëwydh

War vaesow down reverthi
'Bydhez gwolow!' y'n medh Tri,
war leurow gwag tywlezyon
dÿsedha oelez yn-skôn;
kÿweithyanz glan a-henyz
a'vu kynz ez gwruanz byz,
karenzedh y'nn fyrmament
ow' kylc'ha dre'nn oesow lent:
karenzedh dre'nn bledhennow
a'dhûrvydh hedra vo dow.

Ot omma yn Paradhys
dyw garenzedh bys worth bys,
onen arta hag onen,
ny'ezyr onen heb ken;
ny'vern beic'hyow war dhywskoedh,
ny'vern ann Temptyanz nâ'nn Koedh,
Babel, nâ' dow uganzlaw,
Kaethnedh yn Gosen gynz saw:
karenzedh dre'nn bledhennow
a'dhûrvydh hedra vo dow.

Troeyeizi a'dhewisas
tiredh yntre dow vor glas,
dhÿ'ga henath rÿi oelez
dagrennow Tammar ma y'rez;
tan y'n enawsonz, medhav,
a'wythenz dhÿ-vyw dre'nn Gwav,
gwres ha' gwolow dhÿ'nn werin,
santow skov, dÿnarc'h, ha' gwin:
karenzedh dre'nn bledhennow
a'dhûrvydh hedra vo dow.

Skolheygyon hael yn kÿntell
a'dhaeth war-barth nanz yw pell,
koljÿ dhÿ Boll Ann Saethow
y'n kreatsonz kynz, heb gwow;
larjes dhoeth aga c'hÿvoes
rÿ'bazyas dre lieus oes,
dysk, dever ha' didhander,
gwin Oferenn, medhlynn kler:
karenzedh dre'nn bledhennow
a'dhurvydh hedra vo dow.

New Fire[1]

On the deep fields of the torrents 'Let there be light!' said Three, quickly setting out a hearth on the empty floors of darkness; there was pure companionship from ancient times before the making of the world, while love in the firmament was circling through the slow ages: *love through the years will last while there are two.*

Here in Paradise are two loves finger to finger, one again and one, one will never be left alone; burdens on shoulders are of no account, neither Temptation nor Fall are of any account, Babel, or the forty days of rain, captivity in Goshen that was once safe: *love through the years will last while there are two.*

It was Trojans[2] who chose territory between two blue seas, giving to their progeny a hearth where Tamara's[3] tears run; it was fire that they kindled, I say, that they kept alive through the Winter, warmth and light for the common people, rich dishes, welcome, and wine: *love through the years will last while there are two.*

It was generous scholars in a gathering[4] who came together long ago, it was a college that they set up at Polsethow[5] long ago, without a lie; the wise generosity of their common table has lasted many ages, learning, duty and diversion, the wine of the Mass, bright mead: *love through the years will last while there are two.*

Y'nn eur 'mma ot kÿffywyanz
dh'enawi arta flamm sanz,
lenwyl stevellow kosel,
war gÿvamboz gworra sel:
arta y'sÿrc'h serc'h dhigoll,
hudh y'n pÿrth onen hag oll,
ha' leil ann eil dh'y giledh
y'fvydhonz bÿz ammal vedh:
karenzedh dre'nn bledhennow
a'dhûrvydh hedra vo dow.

And now here is an invitation to kindle again a holy flame, to fill quiet rooms, place a seal on a covenant: again will there rise imperishable love, one and all will be merry, and they shall be true to one another to the edge of the grave: *love through the years will last while there are two.*

Benen Bennrudh

Benen bennrudh y'nn telgows un nos,
dasson y'm skovarn ha' gwynz war ann ros:
benen bennrudh kanz mîldir dhÿ-vaes,
benen bennrudh kanz mîldir dhÿ-vaes.

Benen bennrudh y'nn telgows dhÿ vo,
dasson y'm penn ha' glaw war ann to:
benen bennrudh kanz mîldir dhÿ-vaes,
benen bennrudh kanz mîldir dhÿ-vaes.

Benen bennrudh y'nn telgows un nos,
galar y'mm kolonn, awel dre'nn gwydh:
benen bennrudh kanz mîldir dhÿ-vaes,
benen bennrudh kanz mîldir dhÿ-vaes.

Red-haired Woman

Red-haired woman on the telephone one night, echo in my ear and wind on the heath: *red-haired woman a hundred miles away, red-haired woman a hundred miles away.*

Red-haired woman on the telephone in the small hours, echo in my head and rain on the roof: *red-haired woman a hundred miles away, red-haired woman a hundred miles away.*

Red-haired woman on the telephone every day, pain in my heart, breeze through the trees: *red-haired woman a hundred miles away, red-haired woman a hundred miles away.*

Ty ha' My

Dowlagaz down ann nos ma y'sudh,
feuntÿni tywl, feuntÿni kudh,
frozow kelyz hudh, c'hwanz hag own,
dowlagaz leun, dowlagaz down:
hynzi ewn, hynzi kamm,
kolonn veur lamm ha' lamm.

Ann bysyez kryv ha'nn dalghenn tomm,
gwres jolyv gwoez ha'nn tava tromm;
ann balv worth palv ha'nn bys worth bys,
erwi gwresenn yn-dan ann krys:
hynzi ewn, hynzi kamm,
kolonn veur lamm ha' lamm.

Trëyz ow' rima, troez vyw ganz troez
war hen fordh las bÿz kreis ann koez;
gwodhnow war welz ha' kneuz war dhoar,
ponya yn-ghwylz, pawes yn-kloar:
hynzi ewn, hynzi kamm,
kolonn veur lamm ha' lamm.

Feuntÿni trenn y'nn goezwig dhown,
peub lyr ow' lemmyl yn y lown;
anadhlow arav dywedh-dydh,
donz lent ann deil y'nn mynuz rydh.
hynzi ewn, hynzi kamm,
kolonn veur lamm ha' lamm.

You and I

Two deep eyes where the night sinks, dark springs, secret springs, hidden springs of merriment, desire and fear, two full eyes, two deep eyes: *straight paths, crooked paths, great heart beat by beat.*

The strong fingers and the warm grasp, lively warmth of blood and the sudden touching; the palm to palm and the finger to finger, acres of fertile ground under the shirt: *straight paths, crooked paths, great heart beat by beat.*

Feet rhyming, living foot with foot on an old green way to the middle of the wood; soles on grass and flesh on earth, running wildly, rest coolly: *straight paths, crooked paths, great heart beat by beat.*

Vigorous springs in the deep forest, every liquid leaping in its spot; slow-moving breaths of afternoon, slow-witted dance of the leaves in the free minutes: *straight paths, crooked paths, great heart beat by beat.*

Kërynew

Gwonyz y'ghwrug ow thaz
    y bastell dir
yntre'nn bal ha'nn dhreiseug
    un ec'hwedh hir,
ha'nn Gweinten gwlyb pan dhaeth
    ganz oel hag amm,
spusenn vyw dh'y phlanza
    ydh aeth ow mamm.

Y'tovas egin glas
    y'nn gweryz gell,
kyn na'gavse mersi
    ganz gwynzow fell:
ydh ÿmmestynnas c'hwath
    y gelv dhÿ veun,
ha'y dheil dhÿ skorrennow
    a frwythow'n-leun.

Y'ghworrsyn gwenyn owr
    dhÿ gÿntell peill,
drefen haza planzow faeth
    gwenyn a'eill:
bleuzow ha' frwythow palz
    a'dhoe dhÿ'n rann,
avalow ganz kroghen rudh
    ha' kneuz mar gann.

Ha' ladron browt a'dhaeth
    dhÿ stronka'nn dowr,
dhÿ balaz oll dre'nn gweryz
    rag c'hwilaz owr:
ow' rafna tresor ann dhoar
    oll y'ga sorr
y'losksonz ann avallenn
    yn beun ha' skorr.

Mez c'hwath y'koedhas spus
    dre'nn flammow fell,
ha'nn pri a'vu dhÿdhy
    kÿppár ha' kell
ma y'toffenz ynni'n-kudh
    ow' kwortos sin,
lemmyl bÿz y'nn ebrenn
    na's dÿveus fin.

Corineus[1]

My father cultivated his parcel of land between the mine working and the thorny ground one long late afternoon, and when the wet Spring came weeping and kissing, to plant a living pip my mother went.

Green shoots grew in the brown soil, although it had got no mercy from cruel winds: its stem stretched itself out still into a trunk, and its leaves into branches full of fruit.

We put golden bees to gather pollen, because seeding fertile plants is what bees can do: copious flowers and fruit were our lot, apples with red skin and flesh so pure-white.

And arrogant thieves came to pollute the water, to dig all through the soil in order to search for gold: by ransacking the treasure of the earth in all their anger they burned the apple tree, trunk and branches.

But still pips fell through the cruel flames, and the clay was for them like a cell wherein they would grow secretly waiting for a sign, leaping into the sky that has no boundary.

Gwel ann eginow glas
    a-hyz ann ar!
Klyw, yn lev ann awel,
    ann c'hwystrow c'hwar!
Meithrin ann deil a dhowr
    a-hyz ann Hav
ma y'ghwelly omma arta
    gwydh a'ga sav!

See the green shoots along the ploughed ground. Hear, in the voice of the breeze, the gentle whispers. Nurture the leaves with water all through the Summer so that you will see here again trees standing.

Mor ha' Nos

(Dhÿ 'Q')

Y'trovsis yn Kaer Droea treuthow'nn morow
yntre dow dwr rÿ'glywse gwynz ha' kaz;
lanwez dernos a'frapppye war ann darraz,
dassonow koth a'gwske c'hwath y'nn grow;
ha'nn howl pan aeth, y'ghwrae fenestrow melynn
nivera euryow'nn nos a benn dhÿ benn,
sterenn ha' sterenn lent war hynzi'nn ebrenn,
lugarn ha' lugarn vyw y'nn stretow ynn.
Y'ghwoalsis pan vu gworthrec'h, gwwstlow, derai,
ha' testya'n-tdwr dhÿ'nn byz ganz meur a raj,
ha' pan dhÿc'hwele gworc'heul woze trummaj,
yn mysk ann rwth y'saves war ann kai:
haneth y'lennyn ni, yn gwolow tan,
peub geir a'skrivsis war bythyonenn lan.

Sea and Night

(To 'Q')[1]

You found in Troy[2] the threshold of the seas between two towers that had heard wind and battle:[3] the next day's tide would knock on the door, old echoes that still slept in the gravel; and when the sun went, yellow windows would count the hours of the night from one end to another, star by slow star on the paths of the sky, lamp by living lamp in the narrow streets. You watched when there were oppression, riots, turmoil, and bore witness courageously to the world with great care, and when a ship returned after a voyage, amongst the crowd you would stand on the quay. Tonight we shall read, in the light of fire, every word that you wrote on a clean page.

Y'n Medhenz I

Y'ma ewynn donnow ow' kwolc'hi bedh
war vin enyalvor ann parthow gwag.
Y'ma egloes varw (y'n medhenz i)
yn-dan ann tyweuz yw rÿ velynn,
hag y'koedh dydh ma y'fvydh reiz
monez dhÿ rozya worth tu ha'nn lann 'na.

Ke dhÿ gerdhez di, ke, 'sos,
a-hyz bownder yn-nanz dre nywl,
dre nywl ann tes a'goedhas!
Ke dhÿ worra dhâ dhywwodhn
war eskÿrn ann koezwigow beudhyz
hag ot! y'ghwelyth ann enyalvor
yn-lenwyz a lev hen enyvalez.

Rÿ'azsonz aga liwyow
war hynzi c'hwythennow
ma y'fvydh aer, wyow dydhyow
(y'n medhenz i) prêst ow' koedha
hag ommgudh yn mysk ann eskÿrn gwolow
war woelez ann ebrenn nëwydh
yn-honz dhÿ'nn tros ha'nn ewynn.

Ke dhÿ glywez blas
galarganow ha' karolow
gwylaneuz, ke dhÿ sugna
klevow ann enawel yn-dan lemmyl a gowzeuz!
Y'ma leow tywl a-dreiv ann tonnow–
y'kevyr aga thava dre'nn skovarnow
(y'n medhenz i ...)

They Say

The foam of waves is washing a grave on the verge of the wild ocean of the empty parts. There is a dead church[1] (they say) under the sand which is too yellow, and a day will fall when it will be necessary to stroll towards that sacred enclosure.

Just go and walk there, go, boy, along a lane downwards through mist, through the mist of the summer warmth that has fallen. Go and place your soles on the bones of the drowned forests[2] and look, you will see the wild ocean filled with the voice of ancient animals.

They have left their colours on the pathways of bubbles where air, the eggs of days (they say) constantly falls and hides itself amongst the bones of light on the bottom of the new sky beyond the noise and the foam.

Go to taste the flavour[3] of the laments and the dancing songs of seagulls, go to suck the stems of the of the storm beating[4] with conscience. There are dark places behind the waves – they can be touched through the ears (they say...)

Melan Yowan Chÿ'nn Hordh Arall

Yowan 'dh yw ow hanw, Yowan Chÿ'nn Hordh,
Yowan 'dh yw ow hanw, Yowan Chÿ'nn Hordh,
'n-un c'hwilaz c'hwel y'kerdhis 'hyz ann fordh.

Teir phunz y'nn vledhenn, gwobern tânow lowr,
teir phunz y'nn vledhenn, gwobern tânow lowr,
dybri bara syc'h, eva laeth ha' dowr.

Difuna'n kreis ann nos, miraz dre doll,
difuna'n kreis ann nos, miraz dre doll,
gwelez bywnanz dyn 'dan vonez dhÿ-goll.

Kae vyth heb skovarn nâ' than vyth heb mog,
kae vyth heb skovarn nâ' than vyth heb mog,
sawya ow c'hÿweithedh rag prenn ann grog.

Troezya hynz maeneug dre goez ha' 'dreus ros,
troezya hynz maeneug dre goez ha' 'dreus ros,
lemmyl kae ow lowarth dhÿ hanter nos.

Klywez dhâ lev zy ha' lev c'hwath dre'nn mur,
klywez dhâ lev zy ha' lev c'hwath dre'nn mur,
c'hwelez war ow seudhl ha' vodya'n-sur.

Yowan 'dh yw ow hanw, Yowan Chÿ'nn Hordh,
Yowan 'dh yw ow hanw, Yowan Chÿ'nn Hordh,
'n-un oela'n-tynn y'kerdhav 'hyz ann fordh.

The Alternative John of Chenore[1] Blues

John is my name, John of Chenore, John is my name, John of Chenore, looking for work I walked along the road.

Three pounds a year, scanty enough wages, three pounds a year, scanty enough wages,[2] eating dry bread, drinking milk and water.

Waking up in the middle of the night, looking through a hole, waking up in the middle of the night, looking through a hole, seeing a man's life being lost.[3]

No hedge without an ear,[4] nor any fire without smoke, no hedge without an ear, nor any fire without smoke, saving my friends from the gallows tree.[5]

Treading a stony path through wood and over heath, treading a stony path through wood and over heath, jumping the hedge of my garden at midnight.

Hearing your voice and another voice[6] through the wall, hearing your voice and another voice through the wall, turning on my heel and leaving, sure enough.

John is my name, John of Chenore, John is my name, John of Chenore, weeping bitterly I'll walk along the road.

Gwormeul Pezwar

(Dhÿ bezwar kÿweith neb a'dhÿwoalyas penn aga c'hÿzvloedh dhÿ'nn dydh ma y'tdallethas Kÿzgerdh Kërnow, Mei 24edh 1997)

Gwormeul y'n roav dhÿ bezwar
yn eneb kÿweithedh c'hwar.
Kanzvledhenn ha' kanzvledhenn,
gwolow, tywlder, kres ha' frenn,
y'tremmen dydhyow bywnanz
kÿppár hag avon dre nanz:
war-yow y'froz streth amser
yn-fraeththa ez feunteun gler,
glan ha' c'hweg ha' heb difyg,
lammvyw, leveug, down ha' stryg
yn-un leza glasnedh kloar
ha' difuna'nn haz y'nn dhoar.
Dhÿ bezwar y'roav geiryanz:
a'vo gwarthev, bydhez nanz.

Gwormeul y'n roav dhÿ bezwar
yn eneb kÿweithedh c'hwar.
Pedeir c'hwevravon arghanz,
aga hyz ogas dow ganz,
a'froz war-barth yn lanwez
vrastir hy hyz, mor hy lez:
kana, eva ha' c'hwerththin,
moesow'n-poes yn-dan voez fîn,
yec'hyz war-barth y'n evyn,
gwydrennow uc'helder bryn,
yn-tÿrryz forz krinsychez:
a lonkdestenn pyw a'm pez?
Dhÿ bezwar y'roav geiryanz:
a'vo gwarthev, bydhez nanz.

Gwormeul y'n roav dhÿ bezwar
yn eneb kÿweithedh c'hwar.
Ni oll a'dhÿwoal hedhyw
kov rei wiw nag a dhÿ wyw,
nell bryz, nerth breic'h, gwres kolonn,
bri splanna ez ewynn donn,
toth rag gworvetya gwaneg
a'nn gworwel tro ha'nn traeth teg,
mîllev, mîllev ha' mîllev

Praise of Four[1]

(To four friends who celebrated their birthdays together[2] on the day that Cornwall Marches On began, 24 May 1997[3])

Praise I shall give to four in the presence of gentle friends. Century by century, light, darkness, peace and excitement, the days of life will pass like a river through a valley: onwards will flow the stream of time more fluently than a bright spring, clear and sweet and unfailing, leaping with life, vocal, deep and spritely as it spreads cool greenery and wakens the seeds in the earth. *To four I shall give reputation: whosoever would be a summit, let them be a valley.*

Praise I shall give to four in the presence of gentle friends. It is four glistening rivers of silver,[4] their length nearly two hundred, that will flow together in a tide as long as a continent, as wide as a sea: singing, drinking and laughing, tables laden under fine food, it is health that together we shall drink, glasses as high as a hill, the strength of shrivelled thirst broken: for a toast who will ask me? *To four I shall give reputation: whosoever would be a summit, let them be a valley.*

Praise I shall give to four in the presence of gentle friends. It is all of us who will celebrate today the memory of worthy ones that will not wither, vigour of mind, strength of arm, warmth of heart, renown brighter than wave's foam, speed to overtake a breaker from the horizon towards the fair strand, a thousand voices, a thousand voices, and a thousand voices echoing up to heaven, the wind and the way and the sunshine,

yn-un dhassÿni bÿz Nev,
ann gwynz ha'nn hynz ha'nn howlwynn,
gwir na'seiv gwow er y bynn.
Dhÿ bezwar y'roav geiryanz:
a'vo gwarthev, bydhez nanz.

Gwormeul y'n roav dhÿ bezwar
yn eneb kÿweithedh c'hwar.
Dywedhez keudh ha' kÿstudh,
frozez gwin ha' huz ha' hudh!
Kÿvrennyn bara, holan,
azgovow, kÿzgan ha' tan,
gwres karenzedh yntredhon
yn oes y vri a'geiv son,
kÿvoes larj ha' leun dÿnarc'h,
paz didorr eithin, nerth marc'h,
pur dhiamboz y dhanjer
a wreidh ann Noar bÿz dhÿ'nn ster.
Dhÿ bezwar y'roav geiryanz:
a'vo gwarthev, bydhez nanz.

truth against which falsehood will not stand: *To four I shall give reputation: whosoever would be a summit, let them be a valley.*

Praise I shall give to four in the presence of gentle friends. Let there be an end to sorrow and confusion, let wine and magic and merriment flow. Let us share bread, salt, recollections, a chorus, and fire, the renown of warmth and love between us shall be sounded out for ever, generous common table full of welcome, unbreakable endurance of furze, strength of a horse, its jurisdiction quite absolute from the roots of the Earth up to the stars.[5] *To four I shall give reputation: whosoever would be a summit, let them be a valley.*

Marwnaz ann Tri

Myc'hal Yosef dhwr a y sav
a-rag ann grog y'n kanav;
êv a'wonydhe ann dur,
(ann dibervedha kiglomm):
lentr troc'hyyz ann hoarn glan,
kan vorthoel war ann anwan:
ewn ydh o y hynz ha' sur
(ann dial diwyzyg tromm):
kov ha' hanw a'dhûr yn-pell,
dywedh war beub gworthrec'h fell.

Gwow yn-dan y droez y'n stank
Tomas dhyskyz leil Flammank;
y'skoedhye êv breuz ha' gwir,
(ann dibervedha kiglomm):
pledya, dadhla rag ewn vreuz,
erya peub jujyanz pareuz:
frankedh tuz yw kÿvoeth tir
(ann dial diwyzyg tromm):
kov ha' hanw a'dhûr yn-pell,
dywedh war beub gworthrec'h fell.

Jamys Odhlei aeth dhÿ'nn gaz
heb dagr yn y dhowlagaz;
y'paeas y gamp a y benn,
(ann dibervedha kiglomm):
ann gwir er bynn nerth ann byz,
a y renkow skwith ha' fregyz:
dornow dur, pelydhr prenn
(ann dial diwyzyg tromm):
kov ha' hanw a'dhûr yn-pell,
dywedh war beub gworthrec'h fell.

Ann dial darfelleug tromm,
ann diwreidhenna kiglomm,
kov gwerin mar vyw, mar dhown
(azenyzygaeth giglomm):
spyryzow heb maen nâ' bedh,
kas a'gil a garenzedh,
hen henwyn a'feth peub own
(ann attov diwyzyg tromm):
kov ha' hanw a'dhûr yn-pell,
dywedh war beub gworthrec'h fell.

Elegy for the Three[1]

It is brave Michael Joseph[2] standing before the gallows that I shall sing; it is he who wrought the steel (the meat-bare disembowelling):[3] the quenched shine of the bright iron, the song of the hammer on the anvil: straight was his path and certain (the diligent sudden vengeance): memory and name that will last long,[4] an end to all cruel oppression.

It is falsehood that the learned and faithful Thomas Flamank[5] will trample under his foot; he supported justice and right (the meat-bare disembowelling): pleading, arguing for rightful judgment, challenging every ready-made finding: the freedom of people is the wealth of a land (the diligent sudden vengeance): memory and name that will last long, an end to all cruel oppression.

It was James Audley[6] who went to the battle without tears in his eyes; he paid for his feat with his head (the meat-bare disembowelling): the truth against the strength of the world, from his tired and frayed ranks: steel fists, wooden shafts (the diligent sudden vengeance): memory and name that will last long, an end to all cruel oppression.

The hysterical sudden vengeance, the meat-bare deracination, common people's memory so alive, so deep (meat-bare rebirth): spirits without stone or grave, hatred that will recede before love, ancient names that will defeat every fear (the diligent sudden regrowth): memory and name that will last long, an end to all cruel oppression.

Kÿweithas ann Gërnÿwyon, Dy'-Gwoal Byran, 1985

Ot omma vy'n-tdÿvydhyz bÿz y'nn koljÿ un gworthewer,
yn despyt dhÿ geudh kolonn hag yn despyt oll dhÿ'nn gewer,
a'w sav dhÿ Dhy'-Gwoal Byran dhywedh bledhenn bell ha' kalez,
a-rag studhyoryon jolyv yn-dan viraz ha' gwolsowez.

Y'kowsav a'nn hen wydhel war vaen alteur neb a'dreusas
bÿz dhÿ'gan traethow nanz yw pell 'n-un skapya eskar ac'has,
a y grezyanz glan kÿhereug hag a'y gampow eva dyweuz,
a y varthus teudha'nn steunn a'nn maen yn tanzeuz war ann tyweuz.

'Deuz zy dhÿ rÿi dhÿn areith!' dhÿmm y'n medh ann skrivennyades,
'Nâ' mwy ez hanter eur, mar' pleg, hag ÿna reiz dhÿn pawes.
Tamm byc'han gwlazgarenzedh, nebeuz hiraeth, nebeuz c'hwerththin,
hag ÿna dhÿ'nn dywottÿ oll hag onen, 'sos, a'festin.'

Y'styryav fattel dreusas bÿz y'nn gaer 'mma ryb Mor Havren
dhÿ dhyndyl bywnanz kalez, rei nag o studhyoryon lawen,
dhÿ drÿi ann rozow, syc'ha'nn balow, lywyaz ann gworc'holyon,
kÿnuz rag rÿi gwres dhÿ'nn byz a-dreus ann mor dh'y dhanvon.

Y'kowsav a'nn byz kudhyz 'na dhÿ woelez tywl ann balow,
byz maen na'n zÿveus gworwel, le ma y'fveirw ann aer ha'nn gwolow,
a dhwrder ann steunnoryon gynz a golonn leun y'kowsav,
gwormola rei a vywnanz drudh yn peril na'rÿy kalav.

Dhÿ gov y'tdroav ann aerva 'na war vaesow glas Iwerdhon,
pan holyas lu ann vaner Dhu ha' Gwynn a-dreus ann avon,
mez namm na'dÿrr ow lev, ow c'hov dre c'hwetteg eur hag uganz
pan niz yn-tro dhÿ lu a-gÿzgerdh balc'h dhÿ benn un dhownnanz.

Kazoryon vaesow tywl ann glow, kazoryon vraskolonneug,
rÿ'savse bledhenn dhien er bynn ann ryj gallozeug,
yn kÿzgerdh meur yn-tro dhÿ'nn c'hwel heb own, heb meth, heb edreg,
mez oc'h! yn eneb aga feuz y'teudhe kolonn garreg.

Kynz y'trÿc'hy rwthow meur ann kÿvoeth du a'nn downder,
ha' war ann gwelz ma ydh yz ann bal y'c'hwav ann awel dener,
mez degh y'fvu baneryow rudh, ha' dasson Kan ann Dispac'h,
(kÿmmerwc'h gwyth, c'hwi bobl vras, kÿmmerez gwyth ha' brawac'h!)

The Cornish Society,[1] St. Piran's Day,[2] 1985

Here I am come into the college one evening, in defiance of anguish of heart and certainly in defiance of the weather, standing on St. Piran's Day at the end of a long and hard year,[3] in front of lively students who are looking and listening.

I shall speak of that ancient Irishman[4] who crossed on an altar stone[5] right onto our shores to evade a keen enemy, of his pure muscular faith and of his feats of drinking strong drink,[6] of his miracle of melting the tin from the stone in a bonfire on the sand.[7]

'You come and give us a speech,' said the secretary[8] to me, 'no more than half an hour, please, and then we must rest. A bit of patriotism, some longing, some laughter, and then, boy, all and one[9] will hurry to the pub.'

I shall explain how those who were not happy students crossed to this city by the Bristol Channel to earn a hard livelihood, to turn the wheels, pump dry the mines, steer the ships, to send across the sea fuel to give warmth to the world.[10]

I shall speak of that hidden world at the dark bottom of the mines, a world of stone that has no horizon, where the air and the light die, of the courage of the tinners in olden days I shall speak with a full heart, praising ones who in danger gave not a straw for precious life.

I shall recall that battle on the green fields of Ireland,[11] when a host followed the Black and White flag across the river,[12] but my voice nearly breaks when my memory flies back thirty-six hours to a host marching proudly to the top of a certain deep valley.[13]

Warriors of the dark fields of the coal, brave warriors, who had stood for a whole year against the rich and powerful, in a great march back to work without fear, without shame, without regret, but oh! in the face of their fate a heart of rock would melt.

Once great crowds cut the black wealth from the depths, and where the mine is the gentle breeze will blow on the grass, but yesterday there were red flags and the echo of the 'Internationale', (take care, you mighty, take care and be terrified!)

A-ragov y'nn dywottÿ y'ghworryr lieus gwydrenn –
mar hael ann yowynkyon 'mma, mar balz ann nywl y'm kloppenn! –
eskynna 'ghwra ann levow yn-un gana a Vre Gammbronn,
eskynna'n-pell a-uc'h ann pollow dagrow du y'mm kolonn.

In front of me in the pub many glasses are placed – so generous these young ones, so thick the fog in my skull – the voices rise up singing of 'Camborne Hill',[14] rising above the pools of black tears in my heart.

Ann Nown Meur

Pan c'hwave aedh bodrethez
a-hyz tir Elvydh ha'y lez,
sawor vagoeryow difeith
yn anadhl ann strazow leith,
hanazenn Weinten vergloar
pan deudhe gwreidhyow y'nn dhoar,
y'tdifunas haz ankow
yn mysk ann gweryz ha'nn grow.

Dorn poes war ann lasynys
a'wask a'y doar gwoez ha' c'hwys,
a'wask a'y phobl hanter,
a'wask a'y eskÿrn ann mer,
a'wask a'y pharkow kÿvoeth,
a'wask a'y c'hneuz esow noeth,
a'wask a'y c'hres hardegras,
a'wask a'y c'hoseledh kres.

Pluvenn skrivwas a'govath
anadhlow oez, bath ha' bath;
yn fynkow'nn lyvrow-akont,
owr dhÿ duz bywnanz y'n gront:
syc'h pan vo ann parchemynn,
noeth y'fvydh ann eskÿrn gwynn:
worth gwoelez peub pythyonenn
ann grontyanz a'dheu dhÿ-benn.

Dorn hoarn romgrez war golonn
a'wask bolwnzeth dhÿ bonn,
a'wask peub nell a'nn kÿher,
a'wask peub gwolow a'nn ster,
a'wask nerth a vreic'h gledhdydh,
a'wask peub howlwres a'nn dydh,
a'wask froz vyw a'nn gwythi,
a'wask peub gwreidhenn a'nn pri.

P'ann dra yw doar, a' Arloedh,
ma y'kowllÿnk eur, jorneth, bloedh,
devorya kneuz ha' bywnanz
heb gworphenn nefra dh'y c'hwanz?
Ha' p'ann dra dhÿmm yw tiredh
ma y'rÿ a larjes na'hedh
dhÿ'nn dhowdhorn na'n tav jammes?
P'rag dhÿ'nn avleseug peub les?

The Great Hunger[1]

When a miasma of corruption blew the length and breadth of the land of Britain and Ireland, a smell of deserted ruins in the damp valley-bottoms, the sigh of a cool-dropped Spring when the roots were melting in the earth, the seeds of death awoke amongst the soil and the gravel.

A heavy fist on the green island will squeeze from its earth blood and sweat, will squeeze out half its people, will squeeze from its bones the marrow, will squeeze from its fields wealth, will squeeze from its flesh naked want, will squeeze from its peace ill-will, will squeeze from its quietness hatred.

A clerk's quill pen will record the breaths of a lifetime, coin by coin; in the columns of the account books, it is gold that will grant life to people: when the parchment is dry, naked will be the white bones: at the bottom of every page the grant will come to an end.[2]

The iron fist of Roman belief[3] on a heart will squeeze will-power to dust, will squeeze all energy from the muscles, will squeeze all light from the stars, will squeeze strength from a sword arm, will squeeze all warmth of sun from the day, will squeeze a living stream from the veins, will squeeze every root from the clay.

What is earth, that it swallows completely hour, working day, year of life, consumes flesh and life without any finish ever to its desire? And what, pray, is land that it gives of its unceasing generosity to the hands that never touch it? Why does the ne'er-do-well receive every benefit?

Dorn tynn nown war ann pervedh
a'wask a nerth dall tynn bedh,
a'wask ann liw a'nn kroghen,
a'wask serc'h a was ha' ben,
a'wask mersi a'nn enev,
a'wask a'nn byz gwaityanz Nev,
a'wask aer a vrianzenn,
a'wask peub preder a'nn penn.

Poes ann nywl war ann erwi,
skav haz huz heb pluv nâ' si,
kwsk war beub ar ha' glasvaes,
down hunroz a hinon aes:
owr ann tysk war beub trevaz,
arghanz ann gwleuth war beub praz,
hoarn kolonn vab Trev Veilyeun,
gwag peub kist rÿ'vu kynz leun.

Gwynn hag adhvez maes trevaz,
gwynn eskÿrn yn doar wêl kaz.
Ioez aer ammalow ebrenn,
Ioez gwolz yowynk war vîl benn:
gwoluz a'sugn a'nn skubeur
peub sosten dhÿ'nn werin veur,
kowl tânow ha' brows doaral
dhÿ'nn huni a'wonydh pal.

Pan skald losk lymm dhÿ'nn hirdheil
a'nn gwreidh oll a y ben dhÿ'nn eil,
ha' gaza luzw leizblos,
tywlethez yein avél nos,
divoetter a'dhÿw lêmmyn
dre drev ha' nanz, maes ha' bryn,
konsumya ploe ha' kÿvrank
dre beub gworwel oll ma y'stank.

War borva faeth Skubeurynn
pan rowedh ann gwleuth palz gwynn
y'rÿ ann prenn ha'nn alc'hwedh
dhÿ jÿ taw dynyteth vedh:
ryb logow meneic'h Sistel
y'sudh kÿntrevow a wel
ma y'lev ann gwelz kan govow
ann lu tawezeug y'nn grow.

It is the tight fist of hunger on the entrails that will squeeze with the blind grievous strength of a grave, squeeze the colour from the skin, squeeze love from boy and maid, squeeze pity from the soul, squeeze from the Earth the hope of Heaven, squeeze air from the throat, squeeze every thought from the head.

Heavy mist on the acres, light the seeds of magic without feathers or hum, sleep on every tilth and green field, deep a dream of easy fair weather: gold the ears on every harvest, silver the dew on every field, iron the heart of the son of Trevelyan,[4] empty every chest that has formerly been full.

White and ripe the field of harvest, white the bones in the earth of a field of battle, grey the air of the edges of the sky, grey the young hair on a thousand heads: it is wealth that will suck from the barn every nourishment for the great common people, it is thin soup and potato mash for the one who wields the spade.

When a sharp burning scalds to the long leaves from all the roots from one end to another, and leaves foul muddy ash, a dark mess cold like night,[5] it is famine that will burn now through town and valley, field and hill, devour townland and barony through every single horizon where it tramples.

On the fertile pasture of Skibbereen[6] when the copious white dew lies down, the bolt and the key will give to the house of silence the dignity of a grave: by the cells of the Cistercian monks neighbours will sink out of sight where the grass will give voice to the memories of the silent host in the gravel.

Ny'drett gworc'heul plen holan
pan dhrehaedh lu Ponz Ann Wlan,
tuz vaengleudh renk hag ewnrenk,
a-gÿzgerdh er bynn nown trenk:
ydh a ann dydh ganz sosten,
kovaitys worth boez pan len;
ny'vod skath vyth a'nn harborth
kynz del gaffonz peub a dorth.

Gwowdestyon dhÿn a'leveir
nag ÿmmlen styr vyth worth geir,
na'goedh glaw vyth a gommol,
na'gerdhas troez ma ydh eus ol:
ow' testya y'fvydh merthyr
dre weithrez vyw, ober yr,
yn-sur a barth gwiryonedh
(dhÿn ni skolheygyon a'n medh).

Y'kÿwsy hen gloerogyon
a liwyow (dyskyn yn-skôn!)
mertherenzi, rudh ladhanz,
gwynn divroyedh skile sanz:
py liw a'n zÿvydh difyg,
mertherenzi hell ann tryg,
dall fenestri ann krowjÿ,
dyew ann awel, ty ha' my?

Gwynz yac'h a'fes nywl ankov
a'nn henwyn dampnyyz heb prov,
dÿfresa a skeuz Annown
mertherenzi loez ann nown:
ganz tan a barth avorow
y'treilyyn terroz dhÿ brow,
egÿri kistow'nn tresor,
rÿi dhÿ waityanz lez ann mor.

No ship will stride[7] the salt amphitheatre when an army arrives at Wadebridge,[8] quarrymen rank on ordered rank on the march against sour hunger: nourishment will win the day, when avarice clings to food; no boat will leave the harbour before they all receive a loaf.[9]

It is false witnesses who will tell us that no meaning at all will cleave to a word, that no rain will fall from a cloud, that no foot walked where there is a print: a martyr bears witness[10] through living deed, a fresh work, surely on behalf of truth (to us it is scholars who told).

Ancient clerics spoke of the colours (let us learn quickly) of martyrdom, the red of a slaying, the white of exile for a holy motive:[11] what colour for an absence, the slow martyrdom of the ebb, blind the windows of a cottage, the rustle of the breeze, you and me?

It is a healthy wind that will chase away the fog of oblivion from the names condemned without proof, rescue from the shadow of Hades the grey martyrdom of the hunger: on fire for tomorrow, we shall turn disaster to advantage, open the treasure chests, give to hope the breadth of the sea.

Ann Prontor Marthus

Ydh yze prontor marthus
yn Lann Vorwenna c'hweg:
y ganow oll o dadhleug,
y wragedh oll o teg.
Y'ghworte êv a y esedh
war vaen y'nn tonnow fraeth,
ha' garma kan dh'y wragedh
a'sevy war ann traeth.

The Famous Clergyman

There was a famous clergyman[1] in sweet Morwenstow: all his songs were controversial and all his wives were beautiful. He stayed seated on a rock in the swift waves, and shouted a song to his wives who stood on the beach.

Notes

Ann Pennlaw/The High Tide

1 One of the first African-American units in the Union Army, the 54 Massachusetts was formed in the teeth of opposition from many Unionists who insisted that this was to be a white man's war. Refusing to be confined to non-combatant duties, they led an unsuccessful attack on the outer defences of Charleston, where they lost half their strength including their Colonel, Robert Gould Shaw, son of a prominent Boston family. His body was thrown into the common grave with his men. His parents afterwards insisted that their son should continue to rest in the most appropriate place for a soldier, where he had fallen with the men he was leading.

2 The Mississippi.

3 The flag of the Union.

4 *Ann Gwir er bynn ann Byz* – 'The Truth against the World' – traditional motto of the *Gorsethow* or orders of Bards in Brittany, Cornwall and Wales.

Kontrewait/Ambush

1 The Cornish *bownder* 'farm lane' is cognate with the Irish *bóthar* and was probably brought to Cornwall by Irish settlers during the Age of Saints.

2 *Kalann*, the word for the first day – of a month, season or year – is derived from the Latin *Kalends*.

3 An allusion to the Padstow Mayday songs.

4 One of the strangest sights of the Troubles in Ireland has been the intricately-choreographed movement of the foot patrols of the Crown Forces, like a ritual dance but with the entirely utilitarian purpose of ensuring that the movement of each man was covered by his comrades.

Fenestr ann Huz/The Magic Window

1 The television coverage of the Gulf War presented mass slaughter as a video game.

2 Chess seemed an apposite figure, having originated in that quarter of the world.

3 The Cornish word *gwerin*, 'common people', is also used to mean 'pawns'.

4 'Checkmate' is derived from the Persian *shah mat,* 'the king is dead' though the king is *never* taken.

Avalow Mei/The Apples of May

1 On May Day the people of Padstow observe the beginning of Summer with the famous Hobby Horse celebrations.

2 The name Avalon is understood to be derived from *aval* – 'apple'.

3 The refrain of one of the Mayday songs runs *'Unite and unite, and let us all unite/ For Summer is a-coming today,/ And whither are we going, let us all unite/ In the merry morning of May.'*

Hunrozores/Dreamer

1 The Milky Way.

Morreb/By the Sea

1 The expression translated here as 'happy' literally means 'white his world'.

War Woen Las/On a Green Down

1 This poem is written in an alliterative measure, with respectively three, seven seven and seven syllables in the four lines of each stanza, and two alliterations in every line.

2 'The green down' is a traditional kenning for the sea.

An Edhn Tan/The Fire Bird

1 This poem is written in the same measure as the previous one, with a *teirlinenn vac'heug* to close it.

Yn Lannerc'h Gudh y'nn Glaskoez/In a Secret Glade in the Greenwood

1 The traditional name for North Cornwall.

Lywyaz ann Ebrenn/Helmsman of the Sky

1 There is a Cornish pun here, based on the

similarity of the sound between *lyw* – 'helm' and *liw* – 'colour'.
2 Clive Wakfer, an artist from Newlyn.

Ty Arloedh Gwynn/You Blessed Lord

1 While staying with Pawl Dunbar at Liskeard some years ago, I woke in the middle of the night and, because it was so mild, went for a walk in his moonlit vineyard. I had recently been reading one of the poems of the medieval Welsh manuscript, the *Black Book of Carmarthen*, and when I got back to the house I sat down to write these lines.

Karol Nos/Night Carol

1 Andy Davey once asked me for Cornish words to sing to a traditional tune of which he was very fond. Later, he and his brothers formed the group Bucca, which lasted a distressingly short time and released one album, *An Toll yn Pen an Telynyor*/The Hole in the Head of the Harper. This song appears on it.

Gwolow Kynzza Gwener/The First Light of Friday

1 Once you have been bitten by the Country-and-Western bug, there is no cure. These words danced into existence along with a tune that pretty much composed itself.

Amsergan/Timesong

1 Many years ago, I was a student in the same town as Andy Davey, one of the Davey brothers who have so enriched our musical life. We used to meet frequently and turn out songs of all kinds. I had been listening to the song *Tog ejn, tog ajs* from Fiddler on the Roof, and my head was full of feelings about the passage of time. By supper time, Andy and I had composed this lullaby.

An Lew/The Lion

1 The lion in question was a soft toy belonging to a little girl of three.

Myc'hal Yosef, Kwsk yn Kres/Michael Joseph, Sleep in Peace

1 Blacksmith from St Keverne in the Lizard Peninsula, one of the leaders of the Great Rising of 1497.

Jevodí/I tell you

1 *Je vous dis:* in Middle Cornish literature, some characters tend to lace their speech with Breton-accented French. One day this poem bubbled up to the accompaniment of a tune with a bouncing Cajun rhythm.
2 This expression is used in Cornwall to reinforce a statement.
3 In Cornwall, a term indicating gender rather than any particular status. It is quite in order for people who have been married for forty years to address one another as 'maid' and 'boy'.

Lymnores/Painter

1 After dancing, painting is the greatest delight of Anna Eiluned, my younger daughter.

Talek/Talek

1 E.G.R. Hooper is universally known by his Bardic name, Talek, meaning 'Big-browed one'. After the Second World War he opened the first schools teaching the Cornish language as part of the curriculum. They kept the Cornish language a going concern until the new upsurge in the late Seventies. When Richard Gendall emigrated, Talek took on the responsibility for the magazine he had founded, *An Lef (The Voice).* He published it, together with books and pamphlets, with the help of his wife Bertha.
2 Talek published the first regular calendar in Cornish, under the title *Lyver Dydhyow ha Golyow (Book of Days and Feasts)*. In the early years, he often sold it from door to door.

Gelvynak/Gelvynak

1 The Cornish word for 'curlew' is Richard Gendall's Bardic name, reflecting his lifelong interest in birds and nature conservation.

Ow Thaz/My Father

1 My father, Harry Saunders, was by turns a carpenter, a sailor and a priest.

Dowr Byc'han/Little Water

1 The literal translation of *wódka*, the Polish diminutive of *wód*, 'water'.

Saoirse/Saoirse

1 'Freedom', the heroine of Michael Flatley's Lord of the Dance.
2 The date on which the show opened in Las Vegas, with my elder daughter, Gwenno Mererid, in the part.

Kaer Dherw/Derry

1 Suggested by the hymn of Mrs C.F. Alexander and the poem of Colm Cille (also known as Coumba), one of her husband's predecessors as Bishop of the city.

Elynor/Eleanor

1 Eleanor of Provence was promised in marriage to Richard, Earl of Cornwall and King of Germany, but in the event was given to his brother Henry, King of England. It is said that, while still a child, she composed a poem on the story of Tristan and Isolde.

2 I imagined her sailing down the Rhône, like the lovers in *Los Isclo d'Or*, by the Occitan poet Mistral.

3 Richard is said to have introduced the familiar Fifteen Bezants as the coat of arms of Cornwall.

Tan Nëwydh/New Fire

1 An epithalamimium for the wedding of the poet Alan M. Kent and the anthropologist Amy Hale.

2 According to legend, the Cornish are descended from a Trojan called Corineus.

3 The Tamar, Cornwall's eastern boundary for over a thousand years, is said to be a maiden turned into a river.

4 The Augustinian Canons who founded Glasney College, Penryn.

5 The college was set up in answer to a vision that foresaw wonderful events at a place whose name means 'Pool of Arrows'.

Kërynew/Corineus

1 The first of the mythological ancestors of the Cornish. Having defeated the giants, he took possession of the country and gave his name to it.

Mor ha' Nos/Sea and Night

1 The *nom-de-plume* of Sir Arthur Quiller-Couch, journalist, writer and politician. The night and the sea are frequent motifs in his work.

2 'Troy Town' was Q's name for the town of Fowey, wher he lived. The expression 'troy-town' is both an old term for confusion and turmoil, and also for a traditional maze pattern.

3 The entrance to the harbour is guarded by two fortresses, from which in olden times the citizens suspended a great chain to keep out their enemies.

Y'n Medhenz I/They Say

1 The oratory of St Piran at Perranzubuloe is the oldest existing Christian building in Cornwall, and possibly in the whole of Britain. About a thousand years ago the sand-dunes began to encroach on it, and the building has been disappearing and reappearing ever since.

2 The sand along the coast of Cornwall often contains fossils of strange plants. Perhaps this gave rise to some of the legends of drowned forests.

3 Literally, 'hear the flavour'.

4 Literally, 'leaping'.

Melan Yowan Chÿ'an Hordh Arall/The Alternative John of Chenore Blues

1 The seventeenth-century story of John of Chenore tells of a working man who had to go away to find work. (Like many others, I first encountered it in the thrilling recording made by Richard Gendall.) After many adventures, he came back to discover that his wife, despite apparently well-founded suspicions, had kept faith with him. But what if those suspicions had been justified? Chenore is near Treen, in the Shire of Penwith.

2 At the end of each year, John's master offered him a point of wisdom if he would pay back the three pounds. These were, respectively, 'Do not lodge in a house where an old man is married to a young woman', 'Do not leave the old road for the new road', and 'Be struck twice before striking once.' At the end of the three years, the master's wife baked John a cake for him and his wife to break when they would be happiest together.

3 John ran into some friends on the way home, but decided to take lodging next door to them when he saw that the elderly innkeeper had a young wife. During the night, John heard a noise, and when he looked saw the young woman with her boyfriend, a monk, murdering the innkeeper.

4 An old Penwith proverb runs 'There is no hedge without an ear, or down without an eye', to which one scholar appended the comment 'A wise counsel when we speak concerning our governors'.

5 It was John's evidence that saved his friends from being hanged at the instigation of the unfortunate man's relict.

6 In the story, John clapped his hand to the hilt of his dagger, but remembered the first point of wisdom. Entering the house, he

discovered his wife talking to the little son that she had already been carrying when he left. They broke the cake, and found John's nine pounds wages inside.

Gwormeul Pezwar/Praise of Four

1 The four were: John Chapman, piper and storyteller, Pawl Dunbar, vintner, poet and shipwright, Anne Kennedy Truscott, singer; and Maurice Truscott, engineer.
2 Because of the tender youth of one of the four, the celebration was only a hundred and ninety-ninth birthday party.
3 In 1997, thousands of people commemmorated the Great Rising of 1497 by following the route of the Cornish army from St Keverne to Blackheath. During the morning and afternoon of 24 May, many of the company took part in ceremonies and diversions at St Keverne. The party started that evening in a garden at the top of Liskeard, and finished the following evening in a vineyard at the bottom of the town.
4 An allusion to Seth's description of Paradise in the *Origo Mundi*, a fourteenth-century verse drama in Cornish about the creation of the world and its first ages. '... a spring bright like silver/and four great streams truly/running from it...' (O.M. 771–3)
5 An allusion to the legal maxim that possession extends *Ab inferis usque ad celum*.

Marwnaz ann Tri/Elegy for the Three

1 The leaders of the Great Rising of 1497, triggered off by Henry Tudor's attempt to impose an unlawful tax on the Cornish.
2 Blacksmith, of St Keverne in the Lizard peninsula.
3 Scottish hero William Wallace also suffered this barbaric vengeance, after his defeat by Edward Longshanks.
4 As Michael was dragged to Tyburn, he boasted that he would have a 'name perpetual, and a fame permanent and immortal'.
5 Lawyer, of Bodmin, and son of one of Henry Tudor's tax commissioners. He argued that people had the right to resist unlawful acts by their rulers.
6 Professional soldier, who joined the Cornish army at Wells.

Kÿweithas ann Gërnÿwyon, Dy'-Gwoal Byran, 1985/The Cornish Society, St Piran's Day, 1985

1 The society in question was that of Cornish students at University College, Cardiff.
2 St Piran (*Ciarán* in Irish) is the patron saint of Cornish miners. In recent years his feast day, 5 March, has come to be celebrated more and more as a national day.
3 The National Union of Mineworkers had just ended its unsuccessful struggle against the destruction of the coal industry.
4 Piran was a native of Munster, who was forced to leave his homeland after castigating a certain king for his appalling morals.
5 According to legend, the tyrant's men threw Piran into the sea tied to his altar stone, but not only did he fail to sink, he also floated over to Cornwall.
6 Piran was famed for his prodigious thirst, and St Petrock, a saint still honoured in his native Wales, is said to have censured him severely for this. Cornish miners have traditionally called their fellows who had celebrated his feast well rather than wisely 'perraners'.
7 Legend credits Piran with having discovered the art of tin smelting when holding an *al fresco* feast for some of his converts. The black stones he laid down as a makeshift hearth burst open in the heat and the silvery drops of molten tin came out.
8 Dr Loveday Jenkin, biologist, founder of the Cornish Study Centre, *An Gresen Gernewek*, is the daughter of Cornwall's first woman Grand Bard, Ann Jenkin (Bryallen).
9 'One and All' is Cornwall's national motto.
10 Thousands of Cornish people settled in Wales as engineers, seamen, miners and administrators, and Cornish names are common in the Cardiff telephone directory.
11 The Battle of the Boyne, on 1 July 1690.
12 Colonel Charles Trelawny, younger brother of the Bishop Jonathan Trelawny who is the subject of the Cornish national anthem, commanded a regiment in William's army. This seems to be the earliest record of St Piran's cross having been flown in battle. A black flag with a white cross, it has come to be accepted as the national flag.
13 In the South Wales coalfield, the miners returned to work on 4 March. The world's television cameras watched as the Maerdy

Lodge marched back to work at their pit, which would be the last mine in the Rhondda Valley.

14 This song commemorates Richard Trevithick's first successful attempt to run a steam locomotive on the road in 1798. It is almost a second national anthem.

An Nown Meur/The Great Hunger

1 From 1845 till the end of the decade, the potato crops failed over much of Europe. The consequences were severest in the Irish provinces of Munster and Connacht. Most of the population of Ireland subsisted on potatoes, while other crops went to pay the rent. Throughout the Famine, Ireland continued to be a net exporter of food.

2 The economic orthodoxy of the time saw the calamity as the providential functioning of a 'natural' law.

3 The Roman Catholic hierarchy generally supported the established order.

4 Charles Edward Trevelyan, assistant-secretary to the British Treasury, came from an old Cornish family. A moralistic ideologue, he championed rigid financial orthodoxy.

5 The progress of the potato blight was described in great detail in *The Proceedings of the Royal Cornwall Polytechnic Society*, together with vividly accurate coloured illustrations.

6 A townland in Co. Cork which suffered terribly in the Famine Year 1846–47. Its name has become emblematic of the whole calamitous period.

7 In medieval Cornish dramas a character walks with long strides to indicate that he or she is taking a long journey.

8 A town on the river Camel, between Bodmin and Padstow. At one time you could catch a ship for America there at high water.

9 An incident in 1847, in which working people organised to ensure that needed food would be sold at a reasonable price rather than be exported for unreasonable profit. The quarrymen marched down from Delabole, a parish where my father served as priest-in-charge. (The so-called 'food riot', rather than a strike, long remained the preferred measure of popular resistance in Cornwall.)

10 According to the Greek etymology of the word, a martyr is one who bears witness.

11 This symbolism emerged in the Church in Ireland during the Age of saints.

Ann Prontor Marthus/The Famous Clergyman

1 The Revd. R.S. Hawker, the Vicar of Morwenstow, was a famous Victorian poet, controversialist, drug-addict and japester. He is said to have been in the habit of disguising himself as a mermaid and sitting on a rock in the sea.